Collecting Printed Ephemera

COLLECTING

PRINTED EPHEMERA

BY JOHN LEWIS

A Background to **Social Habits** and **Social History**
to **Eating** and **Drinking** to **Travel** and **Heritage**

AND JUST FOR FUN

STUDIO VISTA

Research and production by Griselda Lewis

A Studio Vista book published by
Cassell & Collier Macmillan Publishers Ltd,
35 Red Lion Square, London WC1R 4SG,
and at Sydney, Auckland, Toronto, Johannesburg,
an affiliate of Macmillan Inc., New York

ISBN 0 289 70393 X

Set in Monotype Univers
Printed by BAS Printers Limited, Wallop, Hampshire

Contents

List of illustrations

1870–1935. Printed ephemera can provide background material for a history of railways, or just a decorative montage. The material here consists of cigarette cards 1924–35; a Mortgage Bond c. 1900; a Tourist Ticket Notice 1873; a Railroad Company Ticket 1901; an Audit Office label 1911 and a US Mail train cut c. 1870. 264×203 mm.

1. Uses of Printed Ephemera

Printed ephemera is a term used for anything printed for a specific short-term purpose; such things as a bus ticket, a circus poster, a Christmas card or Valentine, a police summons, a tax demand, a pin packet, a soapflake box, a wine label, a beer mat, a cigarette card, an airline ticket, a train time-table or a travel brochure. There is hardly any limit and although books are outside our field, magazines, comics and newspapers are very much part of it.

Printed ephemera really comes into its own at the beginning of the nineteenth century. Before the Industrial Revolution it was limited to severely utilitarian purposes, such as indentures, licences for watermen, tollgate tickets, proclamations and orders and wrappers for tobacco and tea. The first posters for entertainment appeared in the seventeenth century, as did travel notices which were sometimes engraved. By the mid-eighteenth century the jobbing printer and engraver were busy enough on theatre tickets, trade cards, billheads and labels, wrappers for stationery, pins, perfumes, etc.

In the nineteenth century industry in Great Britain and the USA grew, and so did printing to serve its needs. The output of the ephemeral printer soon far exceeded that of the printer of books. All this throw-away printing was a much more accurate mirror of the times than were the products of the book printer. This still remains true today.

Of all the different things that can be collected, ephemeral printing can cost the least. In fact, it can cost nothing, for it is often the by-product of things one has to buy. Quite apart from collecting for its own sake, so that one builds up a collection of some specific type of ephemera, such as, for example matchbox labels or film posters, printed ephemera can provide the illustrated background to a variety of subjects.

For instance, it can be used for a living visual history of different aspects of the world today or in the relatively recent past. Anyone interested in railways could amass a lot of material to do with their development and history. Cigarette cards, which on the whole had accurate pictures on their fronts and equally accurate information on their backs, could provide a potted history of locomotive design; old railway posters, railway company share certificates, time-tables, advice notes about goods and 'Authorities for Drivers to travel on the wrong line in case of Accident' could help to build up the background material; engraved illustrations of trains on billheads could further illuminate the subject, if not always so accurately.

Local historians could paint a realistic picture of their town, or even just its high street, now no doubt irreparably mutilated, as it looked a century or more ago, from illustrations of shops and other trading establishments that appeared on billheads or in local directories and almanacs. This pictorial material could be given further depth by contemporary auctioneers' posters and announcements of sales of bankrupt stock etc. Such ephemera can be found in local archives and also in private hands. Hoards of old papers are destroyed every year, but once in a while one

FRITH COMMON,
LINDRIDGE.

TO BE SOLD BY AUCTION,

BY JOHN DAVIS

On MONDAY NEXT, OCT. 8th, 1883,

Under an Execution from the County Court of Worcestershire, holden at Tenbury,
and Distress for Rent.—

THE FOLLOWING HOUSEHOLD

FURNITURE

ABOUT 4 TONS OF OLD HAY,

CIDER & PERRY FRUIT

THE PROPERTY OF Mr. C. S. JONES.

Comprising Iron Fender, square Deal Table, Mahogany Card Table, 4 Windsor Chairs. Arm ditto, Iron Pot, Saucepan, Tea Kettle, Tea Tray and Ware, looking Glass, Three-quart Bottle. Towel Rail, Oak Clothes Box, Clothes Basket, Iron Bedstead, Flock Bed, Mattress, Bolsters and Pillows, Sheets, Blankets, and Counterpanes, &c. &c. About 4 Tons of old Hay, and a quantity of Cider and Perry Fruit.

SALE AT ONE O'CLOCK.

Henry Thomas, Printer, &c., Tenbury.

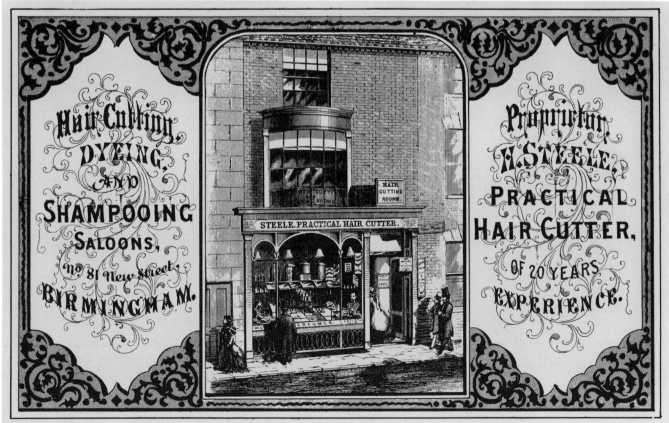

c. 1700 Tobacco wrapping papers from the Bagford Collection and the Collection of the Imperial Tobacco Company. *Courtesy of the Trustees of the British Museum and the Imperial Tobacco Company.*
270×233 mm.

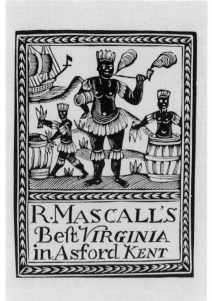

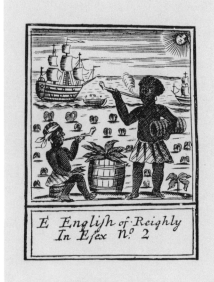

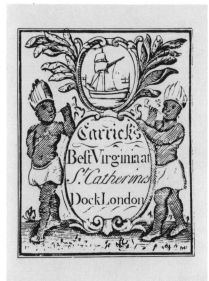

12

may stumble on such a hoard. Lawyers and estate agents provide useful sources of material, and so of course can local libraries and historical museums.

Museum collections of printed ephemera are much more widespread in the United States than they are in Britain, probably because more attention has been paid in America to nineteenth-century social history. Local historical societies are numerous. If for instance, one wanted to do a study of the fishing and sea-faring trades of New England, there is a wealth of material at Mystic Seaport on the Connecticut River, the Peabody Museum at Salem, Massachusetts or the Bath Marine Museum in Maine. Curators and librarians at these museums could no doubt put the researcher in touch with the owners of private collections.

For anyone researching into the history of a trade such as tobacco, a collection of early tobacco wrappers and cigarette packs could give a richly decorative and informative background. Some wood-engraved wrappers in the Bagford Collection in the British Museum show most vividly life on the Virginia plantations at the end of the seventeenth century. A collection of modern cigarette packs and cigar boxes would still evoke much of the history of this trade, for the tobacco trade has always been conservative in its packaging, however advanced its other promotional ideas may have been.

A collection of playbills could supply the basis for the theatrical history of the last two hundred years. Old playbills can still be found, though nowadays rarely for less than £3–£4, or $10.00–$12.00. (A huge collection made by the actor Alec Clunes – something over 11,000 bills – was sold in 1972 at Sotheby's in London.)

Old playbills and no doubt other early pieces of printed ephemera can cost money. To have photographs taken of such pieces in museum and library collections is also expensive. There is an alternative course of action to seeking early material, and this should have much appeal to anyone who is still young. This is to collect today's ephemera, whether it is movie posters, record sleeves, tea cards, car stickers or breakfast cereal packets. In twenty years these pieces of print will be curiously evocative, in fifty years time they will be part of history. This was how Dr John Johnson, one-time printer to the Oxford University Press, began his collection.

Johnson's collection came about as the result of his seeing some people queueing up for a cinema performance. It struck him that just such an instinct for visual satisfaction could be satisfied in other ways – particularly by a new kind of book and magazine illustration. His idea was that everyday printed trivia could show something of the ways and manners of the time and provide illustrations, at least in school books, to an actual day-to-day background. To this end he started to collect printed ephemera. His enormous collection is today housed in the Bodleian Library at Oxford.

A comparable and in some ways more wide-ranging

To be Sold
BY AUCTION,
At the Ulverston Canal Head,
On Saturday, the 6th of August,
1825;
At 10 o'Clock in the Morning:
A QUANTITY OF OLD
CORDAGE,
Sails &c.,
Being the remaining part of the Wreck of the Schooner Sally.

[J. Soulby, Printer, Market-place Ulverston.]

1974 Bullfight poster. Printed by J. Moya, Tarragona. *Courtesy Christian Barker.*
432 × 226 mm.

collection of printed ephemera is the Bella C. Landauer collection at the New York Historical Society. Mrs Landauer, a lady of astonishing vitality, started her collection in 1923 with the purchase from a young man of a portfolio of book plates and other bits and pieces, which she later discovered he had stolen. From that not very promising start, Mrs Landauer went on to make a large collection of bookplates, then branched out into wider fields. Her collection now contains in addition to the bookplates, Valentine cards, trade cards, invitation cards, posters and playbills, lottery tickets, railroad tickets, labels and advertisements for tobacco, beer and other trades.

The Bella C. Landauer collection is housed in a room whose walls are covered with decorative lettered mirrors, shop fascia boards, playbills and notices. It provides a vivid picture of the trade and entertainment history of nineteenth-century America.

Both Mrs Landauer and Dr Johnson intended their collections to be used for serious study. There are other uses which they might have considered frivolous or even improper. The use of printed ephemera for decoration would hardly have appealed to them. Yet what could be more fascinating than a Victorian scrap screen. An assemblage of printed ephemera can also be used to communicate some message, or it can be used to make up a child's game or can even become the basic ingredient of a work of art.

Modern teenagers have revived the habit of using such material, but chromo-lithographed angels, Christmas cards of robins or illuminated pages stuck to the surface of a folding screen are now replaced by decorative record sleeves and pictures of pop idols torn out of magazines, or holiday postcards and anything else that takes their fancy, pasted over bedroom walls. I have known a young bullfighting *afficionado* who pasted the walls of his lavatory, from floor to ceiling with tickets, posters and leaflets advertising *corridas* in every part of Spain. I even heard of an artist who begged some auctioneers' posters with which to line his bath. He then put a gell coat over them and was able to use the bath for its proper purpose. Whilst he lay in it, he could read optimistic descriptions of long since sold desirable properties.

Finally there is the use of printed ephemera as an element in collage. The French word *collage* means pasting or gluing. (It also means clarifying in reference to wine.) As a means of artistic expression, it has come to refer to pictures made up from pieces of printed paper that have been pasted down. Paul Nash described it as 'the art of scissors and paste'. Picasso, Braque and Juan Gris introduced such methods before the First World War, often using materials like wood-grained paper as a substitute for *trompe l'oeil* painting. The Italian Futurists Boccioni and Marinetti used elements of printed typography as a means of shock communication. The most telling use of collage as a means of communication was made by Dada, that anti-establishment, anti-art movement which came

1974 *David Bowie*, collage by 15-year old Margaret Metcalfe.
Courtesy Annabel Fairbrother.
627×113 mm.

1970 *Flowers of the Revolution*: a collage by Gerald Nason. 494×210 mm.

1920 *Bild mit Raumgewächsen*: collage by Kurt Schwitters. *Photograph by courtesy of Marlborough Fine Art (London) Ltd.* 969×680 mm.

into being in Zurich in the middle of the First World War. Dada made use of nonsense in its fight to destroy what its founders considered to be all that was false in contemporary art and society.

The Dada collages made some use of typographic elements. However, the most interesting and certainly the most attractive Dada work was done by the Hanoverian artist Kurt Schwitters, who, because of the romantic charm of his work or perhaps because of his middle-class ways, was described by another Dadaist as 'the Kaspar David Friedrich of the Dadaist revolution'.*

The collages produced by Schwitters often included such pieces of printed ephemera as railway tickets and time-tables, cuttings from newspapers and other apparently irrelevant bits of typography. Schwitters' collages were quite simply works of art, which is more than one could say for most Dada productions.

Kurt Schwitters finally broke away from his class-conscious, politically minded colleagues, saying: 'Art which is related to a certain class of people does not exist, and if it did, it would be of no importance whatever.' This attitude had no bad effect on his collage pictures, which were perhaps the most successful uses of the media ever attempted.

Max Ernst, surrealist and a master of collage, was one of the founders of the Cologne Dada group. He made use of printed ephemera in his illustrations and pictures. His book *La Femme 100 Tetes* (1929) was illustrated with collages made up from Victorian steel engravings of classical females and miscellaneous objects from hardware catalogues, juxtaposed in the most unlikely manner. They evoke most disturbing reactions.

Collage has now become an accepted means of visual expression. A recent exhibition by the English artist Gerald Nason showed some vivid pictures made up from pages of comics. In another more muted picture, called *Flowers of the Revolution 1970*, Nason incorporated scraps of printing, a piece of wallpaper, a printed decorated envelope, part of a picture postcard of Beachy Head lighthouse, some half-tone photographs of soldiers and odd lines of typography saying: 'One of the four executed anarchists' 'Caucasus Poppies', and below some poppy petals, superimposed with a cut-out paper heart, the words 'Made in China'.

Serious motives lie behind such collage pictures, at least in comparison with the Victorian scrap screen or the modern teenage pop culture decorations. But that is no reason for belittling such activities. And sometimes, without conscious striving, these decorative amalgams of printed scrap, on wall or screen, in album or book, can become works of art in their own right.

* Richard Huelsenbeck writing in *Dada: monograph of a movement* Alec Tiranti, London 1957.

2. Festivals and Nostalgia

c. 1870 Valentine cards, lithographed, embossed and cut out. 282 × 200 mm.

In the latter half of the seventeenth century, St Valentine's Day was the most festive day of the year. It was a day for the exchange of presents and a day of celebration. Christmas Day was a much more solemn occasion as a result of Puritan edicts. St Valentine's Day still had some suggestion of a pagan festival, for its date coincided with the Roman feast of Lupercalia, which was a spring festival of fertility rites.

St Valentine was a Roman priest called Valentinus who was sentenced to death by the Emperor Claudius II. In the days before his execution, he became friendly with his gaoler's daughter — a blind girl who brought him his food. The night before he died he wrote a letter to her and signed it 'From your Valentine'. The date was 14 February 270.

Thus Valentine, it is said, became the patron saint of lovers, and, incidentally from those suffering from epilepsy. St Valentine's Day is mentioned by Shakespeare, when in *Hamlet* Ophelia sings:

'Tomorrow is St Valentine's Day
All in the morning betime
And I a maid at your window
To be your Valentine.'

Samuel Pepys mentions the festival more than once in his diary, but his talk is all of gifts with no mention of cards and particularly anonymous cards. By the latter half of the eighteenth century, Valentine cards were coming into use. The early ones were hand-made and written. In the John Johnson Collection there is a little booklet called *The Compleat Valentine Writer,* which was printed in 1794 and sold by T. Sabin, Shoe Lane, Fleet Street, London.

By the beginning of the nineteenth century printers were producing and stationers were selling these cards in profusion. Soon they became highly complicated pieces of print and assembly with lace-like embossing. Artists as famous as Francesco Bartolozzi were designing and engraving Valentines by 1800, with subjects such as 'The Sailor's Farewell' and 'The Lover's Knot'. One of the most prolific publishers of Valentine cards was H. Dobbs & Co, New Bridge Street, London who started working in 1803. He produced some most elaborate embossed cards, including the 'flower-cage' design, which was of German origin. These 'flower-cage' cards were of infinite delicacy. The 'flower-cage' effect was produced by gently pulling on a piece of thread attached to the centre of the design, thus lifting up a gauzy framework to reveal a message written underneath. This involved the most intricate cutting with a sharp knife. Embossing on Valentines was done by placing the paper on an engraved die and pressing it. The lace effect was achieved in the same way, the raised surfaces being filed off.

The introduction in 1840 of the Penny Post in England and in 1845 of the cheap postal rates in the USA gave a great boost to the sale of Valentine cards. About this time, anonymity crept in, which gave an added piquancy to the cards and further accelerated their sales.

c. 1870 Valentine cards, lithographed in full colour, embossed and
cut out.
270×185 mm.

c. 1830 Stockblock of coach with Christmas travellers.
95 × 180 mm.

Many different artists made designs for Valentines, including Alfred Croquill, Robert Cruikshank, Kate Greenaway and Walter Crane. Kate Greenaway's first Valentine set sold over 25,000 copies in a few weeks, for which she received £3. The subjects on Valentine cards ranged from song birds and flowers to lovers, and from railway trains to Halley's comet.

By the middle of the nineteenth century Christmas cards had become popular and the sale of Valentines declined in England, though it thrived in the USA where most of the cards were imported from England. The trade has revived once again but soft sentiments have been replaced by robust humour. Old Valentines, fragile and ephemeral though they were, have survived in surprising numbers, perhaps because they were treasured through the years as tokens of affection from unknown (or known) lovers. The ones shown here come from an album compiled by James Cannan (my wife's great-grandfather) in the 1860s and 1870s, and from a collection of old Valentines made by the Hon. Bridget Sempill a hundred years later.

Christmas cards have a shorter history than Valentines. In fact the first Christmas card was designed and published in 1843 on the instigation of Sir Henry Cole (Felix Summerly). The design, which was of little distinction, was by an artist called J. C. Horsely, who later became a Royal Academician.

Pickwick Papers had been published seven years before the first Christmas card appeared. With the description of Mr Pickwick and his friends boarding the coach, the Muggleton Telegraph, and with everything that happened at Dingley Dell, Dickens imprinted a picture of Christmas that must have affected the character of the season for the next hundred years or so. Christmas cards are a reflection of all this, with their pictures of stage coaches, snowclad landscapes, robin red-breasts and rosy-cheeked children sliding on the ice. The trade boomed. Amongst the first printers of Christmas cards were Messrs Goodall, playing card manufacturers of Camden Town, and also several of the licensees of the print-maker George Baxter. These included chromo-lithographers such as Kronheim, Dean and Sons, Marcus Ward, De la Rue and Raphael Tuck, who in 1893 received the great distinction of a Royal Warrant.

The name Hildesheimer crops up on many Victorian Christmas cards, particularly flower subjects which were lithographed in many colours. This name belongs to the German firm of S. Hildesheimer & Co. who started printing cards in England in 1876 and soon had offices in Manchester and New York. To raise the status of their cards they invited one or two Royal Academicians to design cards for them. Their first attempts were disastrous. Hildesheimer explained how they got round that difficulty:

'Forseeing that designs selected solely by Artists, who however eminent in their profession, had no technical knowledge of chromo-lithography or practical experience of the wants of the Public . . . we were fortunately enabled

c. 1880 Christmas and New Year cards, chromo-lithographed.
The 'Owls' and the 'Three Children' printed and published by
S. Hildersheimer & Co. The 'Kittens' by Raphael Tuck & Co. Ltd.
The 'Moonlight scene' was drawn by the American artist, Astley
H. Baldwin.
325 × 232 mm.

to obtain the valuable services of W. Hagelberg Esq of Berlin, a gentleman of great experience and occupying a foremost position amongst Fine Art Printers, to assist E. D. Leslie Esq and Briton Riviere Esq in the selection of designs.'*

The Victorian Christmas and New Year cards shown here and on page 32 date from the 1880s. They come from an album of nearly 200 cards compiled by Miss Cissie Crane when she was a little girl. The album includes many cards printed by Raphael Tuck and by Hildesheimer and also a couple by W. Hagelberg of Berlin, 'that gentleman of great experience'. One of these is of kittens with moveable heads, the other of an old cottage door and cherry blossom. Hildesheimer's designs here include young huntsmen, owls, flowers and little girls. Little Cissie Crane's album is a fair cross-section of Victorian Christmas cards including snowy landscapes, robin red-breasts, kittens and puppies and views of Arundel Castle, Chichester Cathedral and the Albert Memorial. There are also various religious subjects and a rare comic one of an old man under an umbrella walking into a pillar box in a snow storm. There are hunting scenes and fishergirls, a donkey cart full of mistletoe and New Year cards with 'the compliments of the season' coming from a crossing sweeper and two chestnut sellers and a small boy messing up an artist's painting while the artist is talking to the farmer's daughter.

Old Christmas cards still have a use today. Harold Nicolson, writing about this in *The Spectator* of 31 December 1948 described the calculated actions of a friend: 'The moment he receives a Christmas card, he puts it in an envelope and posts it off to someone else. If the card has been inscribed by some affectionate friend "Love from Pamela" or "With the compliments of Messrs Rickshawe, Court Hairdressers", he does not trouble to erase these inscriptions. He merely adds the words "... and Richard". He contends that this method . . . gives added pleasure to his friends. Not only do they get their cards, but they are left wondering who Pamela may be.'†

Artists Richard Chopping and Denis Wirth-Miller, Blair Hughes-Stanton and Hugh Cronyn and no doubt many more have made just such a use of old cards or printed scraps. After the Second World War there was a boom in do-it-yourself Christmas cards. Artists, designers and typographers found this a pleasant way of making new friendships and keeping old friendships warm. It was amusing to see as distinguished a painter as John Nash drawing a group of truculent Father Christmases coming out on strike or the ex-Bauhaus typographer George Adams doing an elaborate cut-out of a beaming Santa Claus; or the painter Kenneth Rowntree sticking to the same Father Christmas theme in a naïve linocut of Santa

* *The History of the Christmas Card*. George Buday. Rockliff, London 1954.
† Ibid.

1962 Christmas card designed by Fletcher, Forbes, Gill.
221 × 464 mm.

1966 Christmas card collage designed by Kenneth Rowntree.
203 × 152 mm.

c. 1965 Christmas card design cut on linoleum by Kenneth
Rowntree.
145×305 mm.

1969 Christmas card drawn by John Nash RA.
184×117 mm.

c. 1965 Christmas card designed by George Adams FSIA.
215×127 mm.

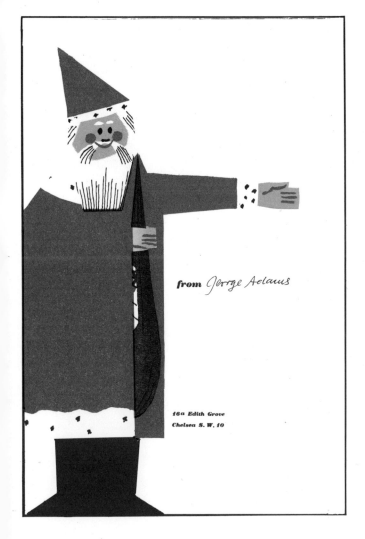

c. 1955 Christmas card using old postcards (1908–18) by Richard Chopping and Denis Wirth-Miller.
140×265 mm.

c. 1960 Christmas card made up from 'scraps' (*c.* 1870) by Hugh Cronyn.
176×228 mm.

Claus as a tug skipper, towing a lighter of gifts and his happily waving family. On another occasion the same artist veered off in a different direction with a stylish Schwitters-like typographic collage. The graphic design team of Fletcher, Forbes and Gill one year spelt out their Christmas message in colourful typographic distortions.

c. 1965 Christmas card made up from 'scraps' (*c.* 1880) by
Blair Hughes-Stanton.
153×120 mm.

c. 1965 Christmas card made up from 'scraps' (*c.* 1880).
90×115 mm.

c. 1970 'scraps' made and printed in England and sold for
ninepence a sheet.
245×180 mm.

1949 Christmas card lithographed by Barnett Freedman for the
London publishers Faber & Faber.
213×330 mm.

c. 1970 Christmas card lithographed by Edward Ardizzone ARA.
145×187 mm.

1954 Christmas card drawn by Lynton Lamb.
125×100 mm.

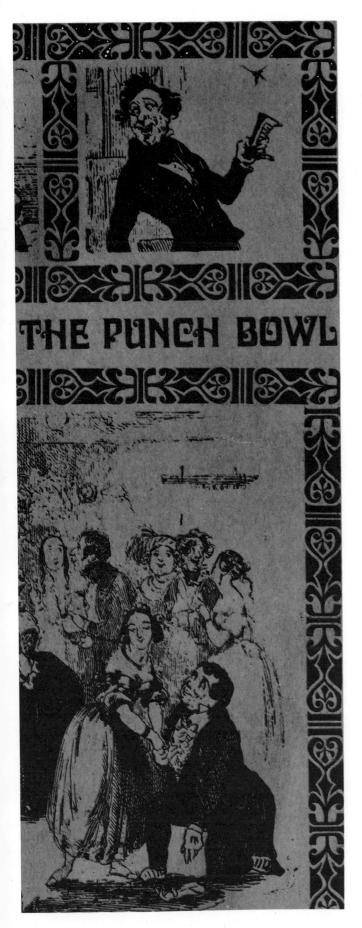

Sophisticated cards have their place, but nostalgia still has much to be said for it. Illustrators such as Edward Ardizzone, Barnett Freedman and Lynton Lamb have produced many charming and evocative designs of Christmas waits, robins and so on. The inspiration comes from the Victorian Christmas card which was an example of popular art. As such it has remarkable staying power. Twigs of holly and church bells as well as robins and snow scenes still evoke Dickensian sentiments and no doubt will continue to dominate Christmas mantelpieces for many a day.

Apart from Christmas cards there are many other forms of printed ephemera that can be used to evoke memories of the festival and particularly those referring to food and drink. Advertisements, posters, catalogues, box covers and labels can all tell a story of good cheer, even of blissful over-indulgence.

In the 1840s H. Magoris, a grocer in the north-eastern town of Hartlepool, sent out a poster headed with the words 'Christmas Cheer' and with a woodcut of an obese boy wishing the customers 'A Merry Christmas to you'. Mr Magoris offered 'Teas, coffees and a lot of prime Wensleydale and Yorkshire cheeses, bought at the Yarm fair'. He also reminds his friends that he is licensed to sell Guiness's Dublin Stout, Burton Mild Ale and other beers. Procter, the Hartlepool printer at about the same time was producing bold window bills for Gin, Rum, Irish and Scotch Whisky (at 2/6d a bottle). No mention of brand names on these – the commodity was all that mattered.

The Victorian Christmas was not all good cheer, at least not for shop assistants, as the spirited lampoon issued at Woodbridge on 22 December 1857 shows. This was about the opening of shops over the Christmas season in which the author of the lampoon refers to 'the avarice, covetousness, cupidity, niggardness and meanness of the shopkeepers'.

What can be more evocative of Christmas feasting than the box tops from crystallized fruits and Elvas plums, or the labels from bottles of Champagne, Madeira and cherry brandy, or colourful cigar box papers and scraps from crackers? A Christmas dinner menu, such as one from the Punch Bowl Hotel at Sefton in Lancashire, would be a reminder of what one hopes was a happy event. The Punch Bowl offered roast turkey and all the bits and pieces that went with it, Christmas pudding with rum sauce and on the cover of the menu reproductions of drawings done by Hablot K. Browne in 1836 for *Pickwick Papers*, illustrating the famous Christmas party at Dingley Dell. A century and a quarter later these drawings still evoke something of Dickens's warmth.

c. 1974 Christmas food and drink: labels and printers' stock block
(c. 1840).
45×85 mm.

SCOTCH
WHISKY

Pure and Fine-flavored, in English-made Bottles,
Full Measure of Six to the Gallon.

2s. 6d.   15s.

PER BOTTLE.   PER GLALON.

JAMAICA
RUM

Pure and Fine-flavored, in English-made Bottles,
Full Measure of Six to the Gallon.

3s.   17s.

PER BOTTLE.   PER GALLON.

GIN

Pure and Fine-flavored, in English-made Bottles,
Full Measure of Six to the Gallon.

2s. 6d.   15s.

PER BOTTLE.   PER GALLON.

IRISH
WHISKY

Pure and Fine-flavored, in English-made Bottles,
Full Measure of Six to the Gallon.

3s.   17s.

PER BOTTLE.   PER GALLON.

1850 Christmas shopping: from *The Illustrated London News*
c. 1880 drawn by Foster and engraved by Edmund Evans.
165 × 230 mm.

1857 Protest Notice, printed in Woodbridge, Suffolk.
215 × 165 mm.

CHRISTMAS
Comes but once-a-Year,
THEREFORE, LET'S be MERRY!

Know all Sensible People by the Presents hereinafter promised to them, that we

Awlfole Tinker-brass O STAND-FOR-NOUGHT,
David Menagerie SCARE CROW,
GEORGE CRICKET BAT HEMP, and
Robert Long-face WAYWARD,

Of GOODBRIDGE, in the County of Silliness, PLUM-PICKERS, not having common sense before our eyes, but being instigated by avarice, covetousness, cupidity, niggardness, and meanness, and having no regard for the comfort of our Assistants at this festive season, DARE, and each of us DURST, in opposition to the intention of all our brother-tradesmen in Goodbridge, aforesaid, and those in Bury, Ipswich, and other towns,

OPEN OUR SHOPS
On Saturday After Christmas Day,

And we have proclaimed this our shame in the public newspapers and by printed bills, and we hereby invite all the customers of other tradesmen to come and lay out their money at our Establishments on that day, promising each and every one of them,

A CHRISTMAS PRESENT
Of One Pepper-Corn!

And we do covenant, promise, and agree, to and with our Assistants, in consideration of depriving them of the only annual enjoyment they can have of visiting their Friends at Christmas, to give them **Two full clear days' Holiday on the 29th and 30th of February next.**

Given under our sugar-sticks, this 22nd day of Dec., 1857,

Witness THOMAS COCKCROW,}　　A. T. O. STAND-FOR-NOUGHT,　G. B. HEMP.
　　　　　WILLIAM REYNARD. }　　D. M. SCARECROW,　　　　　　R. L. WAYWARD.

CHRISTMAS  CHEER!!

H. MAGORIS

Begs to thank his Friends and Customers for their Liberal Support since his removal to his New Premises in Middlegate, and to assure them that nothing shall be wanting on his part to merit a continuance of their favours. He also invites those who have not as yet given him a trial to do so, and then judge for themselves. As it is not expedient to price every description of goods, he will merely quote a few prices of the leading articles :---

TEAS,	COFFEES,
from 1s. 4d. to 4s. Per lb.	from 10d. to 1s. 6d. Per lb.

Sugars and every other article in the grocery trade, the same as other houses. Particular attention is requested to his stock of NEW FRUITS, they being of the finest description. A lot of Prime

Wensleydale & Yorkshire

CHEESES

Purchased at Yarm Fair; and, as he purchases every article for Cash, he is enabled to offer them at the lowest possible prices.

Agent for ARTHUR GUINNESS, SON, and Co's. DUBLIN STOUT
    (Half Barrels to suit families), £1 5s.

	Quarts.	Pints.	½-pints.
In Bottles (per dozen) at- - - - - -	5s. 0d.	3s. 0d.	2s. 0d.
Agent for BASS & Co's. BURTON MILD and BITTER BEER, in Wood and Bottles -	6s. 0d.	3s. 6d.	2s. 3d.
Agent for JEFFREY & Co's. EDINBRO' ALE	5s. 0d.	3s. 0d.	2s. 0d.

Agent for COURAGE & Co's. LONDON STOUT, in Casks only. This
    Stout is principally to supply the Trade.

A Stock of KENDAL ALE, in 9-gallon Casks, always on hand (to suit private families) at prices as follow :---10s. 6d., 12s., 13s. 6d., and 15s., for very strong.

A Trial is earnestly Solicited.

B. T. ORD, MACHINE PRINTER, &c., HIGH STREET, HARTLEPOOL.

c. 1880 New Year cards, lithographed in full colour from Miss
Cissie Crane's album.
296×230 mm.

c. 1965 'Tramway': board game designed by C. French and
C. Babcock. Printed at the Norwich School of Art on two sheets.
421 × 596 mm.

1856 'Edmiston's Crimean Outfit': advertisement from the first
edition of *Little Dorrit* by Charles Dickens.
205 × 125 mm.

EDMISTON'S
CRIMEAN OUTFIT,
£18 18s.

Comprising the following requisites for Officers proceeding to the seat of War, viz.:—

Waterproof Cape and Hood.	Bucket and Bason.
„ Camp Boots.	Brush Case.
„ Ground Sheet.	Lantern.
Folding Bedstead.	Havresack.
Mattrass and Pair of Blankets.	Pair of Pack Saddle Trunks, with
Canteen for Two Persons.	Straps and Slinging Irons
Sponging Bath.	complete.

Attention is respectfully invited to

EDMISTON'S WATERPROOF WINTER CAPE, WITH HOOD,
CAMEL-HAIR LINED.

PAIR of BULLOCK TRUNKS, forming BEDSTEAD,
With Straps and Slinging Irons, complete in one, £6 10s.

PORTABLE WATERPROOF PATROL TENTS,
Weighing 10 lb., price £2 2s.

PORTABLE INDIA-RUBBER BOATS,
On View, same as used in the Harbour of Balaklava.

THE POCKET SIPHONIA,
OR WATERPROOF OVERCOAT,

Weighing 10 oz. Price, according to size, 40s. to 50s.; all silk throughout, 50s. to 60s.

Stout Siphonias, 25s. to 35s. Overalls, 10s. 6d. Yacht Jackets, 18s. 6d.
Reversible Alpacas, 35s. each, suitable for Clergymen.

NOTICE.—NAME & ADDRESS STAMPED INSIDE. NONE OTHERS ARE GENUINE.

EDMISTON & SON, No. 69, STRAND, LONDON.

Board games like Ludo (Parcheesi) and Snakes and Ladders were perennially popular. The Bethnal Green Museum in London has a fine collection of such games. One is called 'The New Game: Virtue Rewarded and Vice Punished'. A notice that goes with it says: 'It is designed with a view to promoting progressive improvement of the juvenile mind, and to deter them from pursuing the dangerous Paths of Vice.' It is, in spite of its intimidating subject, prettily hand coloured and was published by Wm Darton in London in 1818. Another board game on view at Bethnal Green is a version of Lotto and another the Race Game Minoru, named after King Edward VII's Derby winner of 1909. In the USA there are various toy collections including the Margaret Woodbury Strong Museum at Rochester, N.Y., which has a fine collection of toys, games and doll's houses.

There are other examples here of nineteenth-century printed ephemera such as toy bricks with printed designs, a 'Fancy Bazaar' with coloured prints of aristocratic traders, sets of penny toys in matchboxes with printed covers and a beautiful Toy Catalogue, produced by the firm of Biberack of Nuremburg *c.* 1836, with engraved and hand-coloured illustrations of toys, dolls, musical instruments and dolls' house furniture.

Tramway is a modern version of a board game. This was designed in the 1960s by Chris French and Cheryl Babcock while they were students at the Norwich School of Art. The illustrations were largely drawn from ephemeral printing and include railway and tram tickets, posters (a nice nineteenth-century one for the Newcastle Races), and photographs and drawings. There are clearly endless possibilities for creating board games with the use of printed ephemera. And not only board games. The various varieties of 'War Games' could use such cigarette cards series as John Players' 'Army Corps and Divisional Signs' or the same company's 'Regimental Uniforms', or illustrations torn out of magazines, reproductions of old war posters or even cut-out figures of military uniforms from breakfast cereal packets. The print of a camouflaged combat soldier at the head of the next page is one of a series of wall sheets produced in Beirut to popularize the Lebanese Army. Such material could be used not only for 'War Games' but as background material for articles, exercises and theses about war.

c. 1970 'War Games'. An assembly of printed ephemera including
a Lebanese wall sheet, cut-out figures of Yeomanry and Horse
Guards uniforms, reproductions of First World War posters, a 1918
Christmas card from Paris and cigarette cards.
560 × 363 mm.

c. 1845 'Nuts to Crack': broadsheet published by R. Macdonald, Clerkenwell, London. 507 × 377 mm.

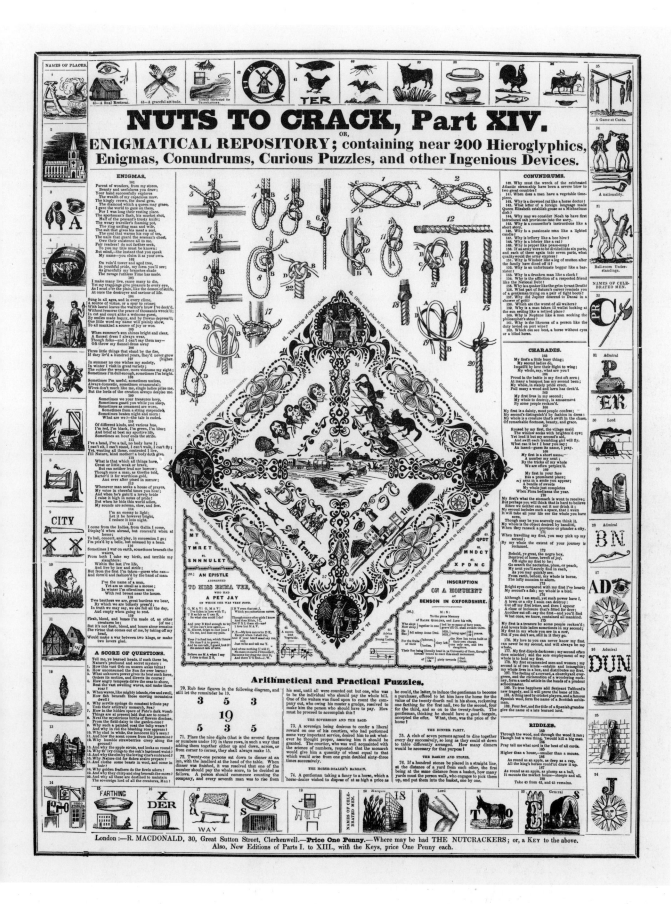

The Christmas pantomime is a recurring annual feature. The origin of the pantomime goes back to Roman times. Our present-day pantomimes can be traced back to the 1730s; they were based in part on Italian comedies and the *dénouement* was often followed by an elaborate transformation scene after which the broad slapstick comedy of Clown and Pantaloon was followed by a ballet performance featuring Columbine and Harlequin. The Clown became increasingly popular during the nineteenth century and one of the most famous was Joseph Grimaldi who was long associated with the pantomime *Mother Goose*, which was first put on at Covent Garden in 1806.

Soon every kind of fairy story and legend was used as a basis for the slender plots of these pantomimes. Stories from Grimm, Perrault and the *Arabian Nights* were plundered.

In the 1870s *Lalla Rookh* or *Harlequin, the Princess, the Peri and the Troubadour* was shown at the Theatre Royal, Greenock. This decorative bill, printed in red and green, was set up with a over dozen different typefaces. At the bottom is printed 'and one that all children who have behaved well during the past year, should be indulged with a sight of!' The *Aladdin* poster was printed by silkscreen a century later in garish Day-Glo inks, (see page 48).

Circuses were as much a part of the Christmas scene as the Pantomime. Today they occur more rarely and the days of Bertram Mills's great circus at Olympia in London are over. The early posters such as the one for Manders' Menagerie, which dates from 1873, were as remarkable for their typography as they were for the variety of the acts they described.

Manders' Menagerie, with its 'Matchless group of twenty lions, four performing elephants, Lapland wolves, blue-faced gorillas, cheetahs, leopards etc' used to arrive at the outskirts of provincial towns and then form up with a 'Grand Procession headed by the Gorgeous Golden Band Chariot, drawn by four elephants, two camels, two dromedaries, containing the All-England Champion Brass Band'. The entrance cost one shilling, children under ten years sixpence and 'the labouring classes' sixpence.

Outings to the pantomime or the circus, for those who could afford to go, would only occupy one or two evenings in the Christmas season. The rest of the holiday time was taken up with home entertainment. Parlour games such as a series of sheets called *Nuts to Crack* were highly popular. These sheets, costing one penny each, usually contained an elaborate rebus in the centre, surrounded by conundrums, enigmas, charades, puzzles and riddles.

c. 1870 Pantomime poster. Marked up copy with *Cinderella* for
Lalla Rookh Hartlepool for Greenock and other substitutions.
506×252 mm.

1873 Poster. Printed by Henry Greenwood, Liverpool.
660×374 mm.

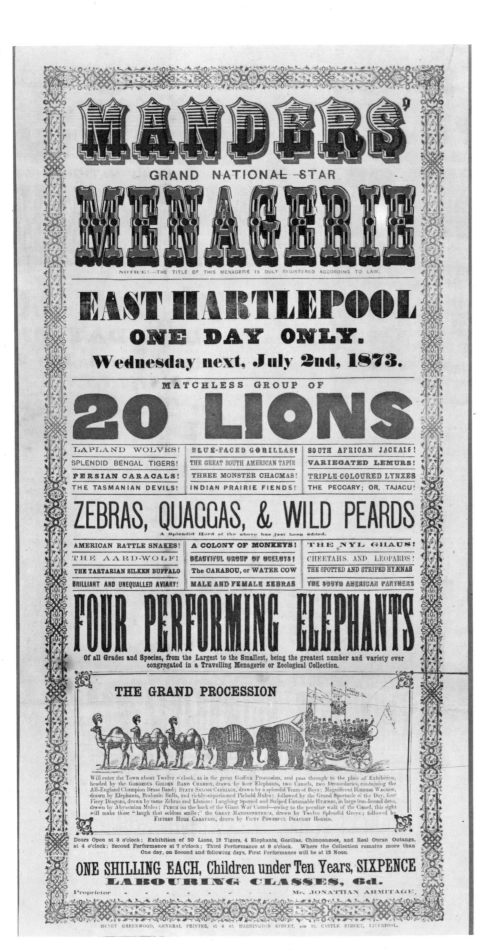

For the grown-ups in Victorian times, throughout the year there were concerts, both sacred and secular. In 1838, Miss Hill, the blind singer 'of the London and New York Concerts and Sacred Music Society' announced in a robust black type on a yellow paper a 'Concert of Sacred Music to be held at the Unitarian Chapel, Springfield, Mass.' Fifty years later, printed in pink and black from even more robust wood letters, but still on yellow paper, Springthorpe announced his 'Exhibition and Promenade Concerts' to be held at the Mechanics Institute, Hull. Corrections in ink to this bill indicate that a certain Mr Tonelli is advertising in the same manner a concert at the Temperance Hall, Hartlepool.

The verve and vitality of the nineteenth-century bills such as these has never been equalled, though pastiche Victorian typography recurs fairly frequently. The 1972 bill for the Coventry Cathedral 'Salute to the 1870s' is a successful attempt; the National Portrait Gallery's bill from the previous year for an exhibition of Victorian Music Covers is an even more exuberant effort, printed in red and black on a yellow paper.* This bill takes us back once again to the times when people had to entertain themselves. Nearly every cottage had a piano in the front room. On Saturday nights and Sunday afternoons young and old would gather round the upright Broadwood and sing ballads and sentimental songs. The demand for the sheet music was enormous and as a lively record sleeve helps to sell the pop records of today, so colour-lithographed covers increased the sale of sheet music. The covers varied from illustrations of the songs to portraits of the music-hall stars who had made them famous. Albums of these forgotten songs can still be found, with the covers bound into them. The covers are usually more interesting than the music!

* Pages 152–3

c. 1885 Music cover lithographed by Stannard & Son.
340 × 240 mm.

1838 Concert bill printed at Springfield, Mass.
410×287 mm.

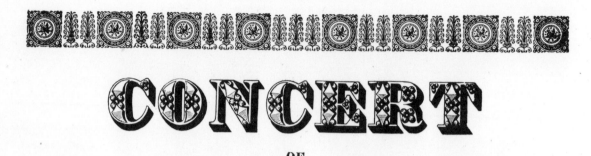

CONCERT

OF

Sacred Music.

Miss HILL (of the London and New York Concerts and Sacred Music Society) begs leave to announce to her friends and the public that a performance of

CLASSICAL SACRED MUSIC

will take place at the UNITARIAN CHURCH, on *Monday Evening, the 16th inst.*---To commence at 8 o'clock, precisely.

Organist & Conductor,---Mr. W. H. COPE,
(late Organist of the Moravian Church in New York)

Miss HILL deems it proper to state, that she has from infancy endured the *privation of sight.*

PROGRAMME.

PART 1.	PART 2.
OVERTURE—Messiah, *Handel.*	ORGAN VOLUNTARY—Mr. Cope--Extemporaneous.
DUET. Miss Hill and Mr. Cope---Forsake me not. *Spohr.*	ARIA. Miss Hill—But thou did not leave his soul in Hell. *Handel.*
ARIA. Miss Hill----A Holy Spirit loving goodness. *Romberg.*	RECIT.) Miss Hill—Ye sacred Priests.
ORGAN VOLUNTARY. Mr. Cope—Adeste Fideles, with Var's. *Adams.*	ARIA.) Farewell ye limpid springs. *Handel.*
RECIT.) Miss Hill--Comfort ye my people.	ORGAN DUET. Miss Hill and Mr. Cope--The marvel'ous work. *Haydn.*
ARIA.) Ev'ry valley shall be exalted *Handel*	ARIA. Miss Hill—Let the bright Seraphim. *Handel.*
DUET. Miss Hill and Mr. Cope—"Shew us thy Mercy." *Boyce.*	ORGAN VOLUNTARY—Mr. Cope.

☞TICKETS, 50 cents each, to be had at the Hotels and Bookstores. *Springfield, July 14th, 1838.*

c. 1885 Music cover lithographed by Stannard & Son.
340 × 255 mm

c. 1885 Music cover lithographed by K. Laby.
340×243 mm.

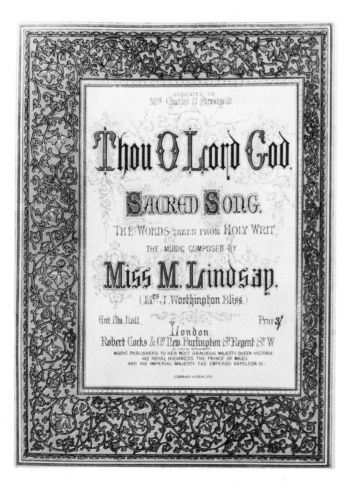

In the days before radio and television those who were not musical and did not enjoy word games could still entertain themselves with looking at their collections of pressed flowers or postcards. The London Stereoscopic Company in 1856, in the second number of Dickens's *Little Dorrit,* advertised the 'Lenticular Stereoscope'. This was an optical device whereby a three-dimensional appearance could be produced from photographs. The advertiser stated that 'You will find it a delightful companion in solitude and for social and domestic gatherings, an unfailing source of intellectual enjoyment. With it no company can ever be *dull* – the themes of conversation it suggests are as boundless as the pleasure it affords.'

The next stage for the visually minded was the magic lantern with hand-coloured glass slides, some of which had parts that moved. I can remember seeing a view of a Welsh valley and a viaduct, over which a train went puffing. Another moveable slide was of a man in a nightcap asleep and snoring. A rat ran from under the bed up over the coverlet and into his open mouth. This could be repeated *ad nauseam.*

1856 Advertisement from the paper cover of the 2nd number of
Little Dorrit by Charles Dickens.
152×98 mm.

1877 Entertainment poster.
215×135 mm.

1868 Exhibition leaflet, printed by J. Procter, Hartlepool.
190×122 mm.

THE LONDON

STEREOSCOPIC COMPANY,

54, CHEAPSIDE (Two Doors West of Bow Church),

AND

313, OXFORD STREET,

(CORNER OF HANOVER SQUARE, TWENTY DOORS WEST OF REGENT STREET.)

"Seems Madam! Nay, it IS!" Hamlet

10,000 GROUPS & SCENES

FROM NATURES LOVELIEST NOOK & DELL
TO ITS GRANDEST ALPINE GLACIER.

Particulars of Subjects, &c., are in the annexed Catalogue.

AN ENTERTAINMENT

Will be given in the

Primitive Methodist Chapel,

KELLOE,

On Saturday, February 3rd, 1877,

ILLUSTRATED BY

DISSOLVING
VIEWS
AND
LIME-LIGHT

SUBJECTS:—

Pilgrim's Progress—Life of Christ—
Dear Father, Come Home—Ship on
Fire, with other views for Children.

Doors open at 6.30., commence at 7 o'clock.

Part of Proceeds to go towards Chapel.

Come in Good Time to obtain Good Seats

ADULTS, 6d. CHILDREN 3d. each.

Hartlepool: J. Procter, Printer by Steam Power.

Hartlepool Temperance Society's

BAND OF HOPE

ARRANGEMENTS HAVE BEEN MADE FOR AN

EXHIBITION

OF A SPLENDID SERIES OF

DISSOLVING VIEWS,

MOVING FIGURES, &c., &c.,

On Wednesday Evening, Dec. 23rd, 1868,

AS EXHIBITED BEFORE THE

ROYAL FAMILY

And to Hundreds of Thousands of all classes of Society at the

ROYAL POLYTECHNIC, LONDON.

The effects are produced by a pair of first class Lanterns, and
(when time and space will permit) with the beautiful

OXYCALCIUM LIME LIGHT.

There are upwards of 60 different Views, such as Summer changing to Winter, with falling snow effect; The Harvest Field, with
mechanical moving figure in the foreground; Farm House, with
moving Goat and Child; interior of same, Lady playing Piano-
forte, &c.; to be followed by a number of beautiful Mechanical
MARINE VIEWS, illustrating the pleasures and perils of a
seafaring life—Moving Ships by Day and Moonlight. Morning—
Ship outward bound, fine weather. Evening—Ship in danger of
being swamped by a large waterspout—beautiful Rainbow Effect
in this scene. Night—A dreadful Storm, with startling Lightning
effects; ship struck by the same; takes fire; crew form raft;
ship sinks. Morning—Sail in sight; all saved. After which a
number of very beautiful scenes, consisting of Grottos, Caves,
and Sea Views, with Moving Water by Day and Moonlight.
The above cannot fail to be both interesting and instructive to
young and old.
The whole to conclude with a number of

COMIC MECHANICAL FIGURES,

which always calls forth the liveliest merriment from the little
ones, and provokes pleasant jokes from the adults.

TO COMMENCE AT HALF-PAST SEVEN O'CLOCK.

ADMISSION:—ONE PENNY.

Hartlepool: J PROCTER, Printer by Steam Power. 12,537.

c. 1960 Pantomime poster printed in Day-Glo colours.
508 × 320 mm.

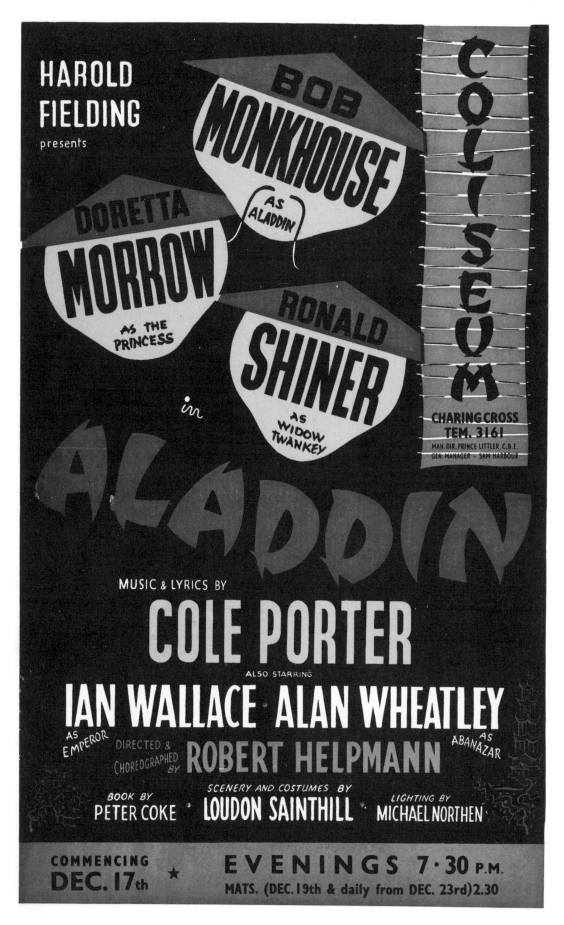

c. 1962 Film Society posters, designed and printed at the Royal
College of Art, London.
712×308 mm.

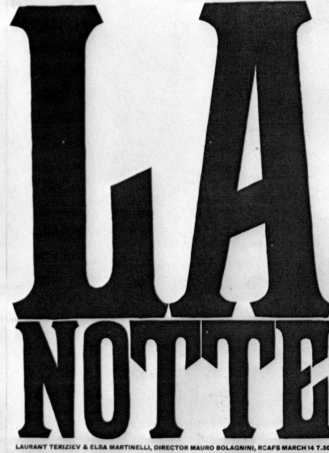

LAURANT TERIZIEV & ELSA MARTINELLI, DIRECTOR MAURO BOLAGNINI, RCAFS MARCH 14 7.30

Marilyn with Monroe
ROYAL COLLEGE OF ART FILM SOCIETY. FEBRUARY 28th, 7.30 pm

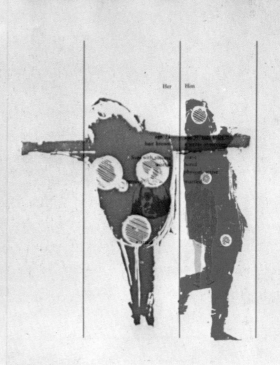

1971—4 Wall decoration made up from the sleeves of 'Pop'
records.
Each approximately 310×310 mm.

opposite page 4

1877 Entertainment poster.
250×185 mm.

HUTTON HENRY
Church Missionary Society.
A LECTURE
In aid of the above Society, will be given in the Church,
On Tuesday Evening, Jan. 30, 1877,
BY THE
REV. W. MASON
MISSIONARY FROM AMONG THE
North American Indians.
TO COMMENCE AT 7 OCLOCK.
Monk Hesleden, January 23rd, 1877.
Hartlepool: J. PROCTER, Printer by Steam Power.

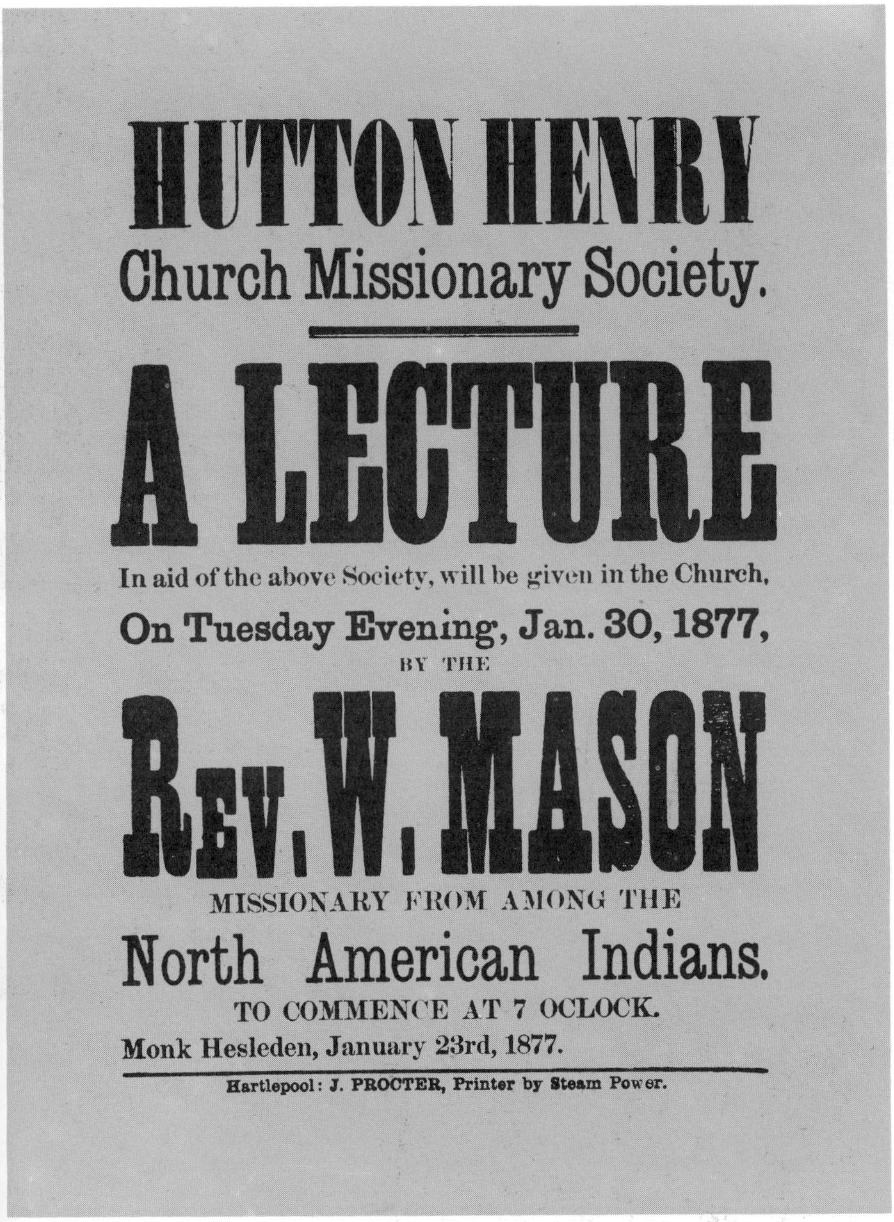

The magic lantern soon became the main support of the professional lecturer, whether he was giving 'A Grand and attractive Phantasmagorial Exhibition' (whatever that may have been) or describing the activities of the Society for the Propagation of the Gospel or the Church Missionary Society, with inevitable pictures of South Sea islanders miserably over-dressed in 'Mother Hubbards'.

c. 1930 Record sleeve
230 × 230 mm.

The mid-twentieth-century equivalent of the magic lantern is the home or club movie with linked stereophonic sound. Most schools have their film societies and produce their own posters for their film shows. The posters for *La Notte* and *Some like it Hot* were produced in the early 1960s at the Royal College of Art. Such posters are a reflection of the taste of a particular year, as well as of the skills of the students who produced them. Even more so are the pop record sleeves – more representative of a moment in time because of the transitory fame of so many pop stars. The first covers for the early records by the Beatles are now historical documents. No doubt the record sleeves of David Bowie, Charles Asnavour, John Denver, or Jimi Hendrix in twenty years time will be regarded in the same light, or with blank wonder as to who they were, and how or why they turned on this generation.

These sleeves are pop art as well as aids to selling pop music. They have a persuasive vitality which makes them live in their own right. They are amongst the most evocative of today's printed ephemera.

1971 Record sleeve.
177×177 mm.

1972 Record sleeve.
177×177 mm.

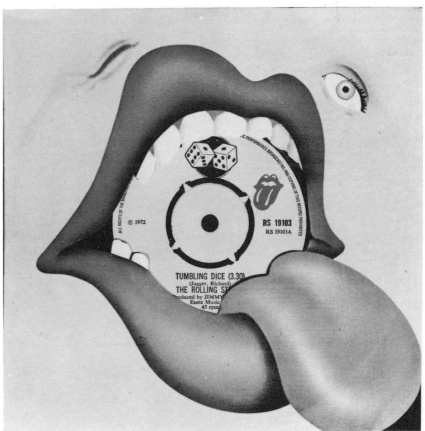

c. 1900 Accident insurance leaflet.
225×146 mm.

c. 1900 Zeeland Steamship Company advertisement, lithographed
by L. van Leer, Amsterdam.
170×67 mm.

1914 Postcard 'Strand Boulevard' at Scheveningen.
89×138 mm.

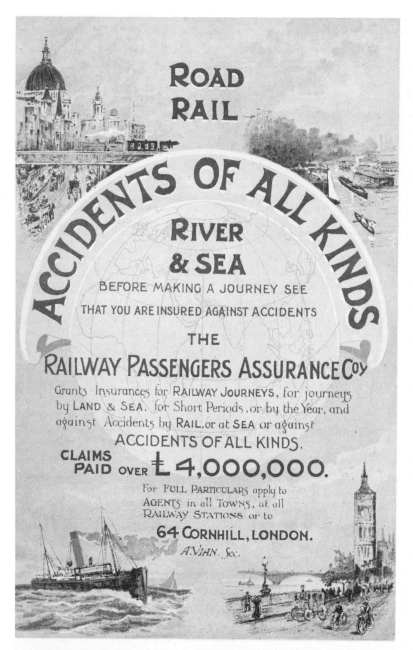

3. Holidays Abroad and the Grand Tour

Picture postcards provide the most obvious form of ephemeral printing with which to recall memories of holidays. The card from Scheveningen was posted to England on 15 July 1914 — just under three weeks before the outbreak of the First World War.

Long before picture postcards became fashionable, travellers were setting out on continental holidays on what has become known as 'The Grand Tour'. This was a somewhat more hazardous holiday than the modern 'package tour' of the travel agents and holiday operators. From 1822 the resolute traveller at least had as a guide and interpreter Madame Stephanie-Félicité de Genlis, a literary lady of some pretensions, who had been governess to the children of Philippe-Egalité, Duc d'Orleans. Madame de Genlis came to the aid of the tourist with her phrasebook *The Traveller's Companion for Conversation*, written in English, German, French, Italian, Spanish, and Russian. Her conversational gambits go far beyond the realms of 'Where is the pen of the postillion's aunt?'. For instance, in reply to a question 'What sort of provisions should I take?' she rattles off a list that includes 'lemons, good prunes (two wholesome aliments particularly at sea), barley grains, rice, vermicelli, good honey, sugar, cooking syrups, conserves, portable soups (which is to be had genuine and good at Berlin and Hamburgh; it keeps a long time). Finally if you are going upon a long voyage, you must take along with you a stock of live poultry, beer, porter and wine. Don't forget to provide yourself with sheets and bedcovers.' She is never at a loss. After the carriage has been upset, her companion says 'The coachman has fallen into a swoon; he has broken an arm, a leg; he has got a large boil upon his head. Ought we not to apply a piece of money to make it quite flat?' Madame de Genlis replies: 'By no means, your proposal is preposterous!'

As far as recording the tour by means of printed ephemera, there was plenty of material in the form of billheads from taverns, wrappers and boxlids from pharmacists, grocers and other shops. There were tickets from coach companies and for tollgates and packet boats. There were playbills and other notices and so on.

The two bills advertising 'The Union' and *Messageries Royales* were probably printed in the 1830s. Both companies rendezvous at the White Bear in Piccadilly. The 'Union' has three coaches a day going to Dover and back and *Messageries Royales* only two, but you could be booked right through to Paris by the *Messageries Royales* for £3.14.0 for an inside seat in their 'New English Diligences'. If Madame was tired the family could break their journey at the Hotel de l'Ange at Breteuil, seven leagues from Amiens. In his advertising card, M. Petigny-Despeaux offers the travellers 'All convenience, neatness and security they can desire — and comodious stables.' As the tour continued hotel cards and billheads were collected at Haarlem, Cologne, Baden-Baden, Goslar, Munich, Geneva, Vienna and Sestri. They may have shopped in Paris, where following Madame de Genlis's advice, they would have bought stores and also perfumes.

This material, however, is as nothing compared to the mass of printed matter that the modern traveller could assemble in a weekend trip or a couple of weeks' holiday abroad.

At the turn of the century as holidays abroad became a part at least of English and American middle-class life, insurance companies and shipping lines increased their advertising. The Railway Passengers Assurance Company offered (on the back of their leaflet) £500 and £3 weekly allowance for disablement for a sixpence insurance ticket, for accidents on 'cross passages in the United Kingdom and for journeys to the Continent'. On the front of the leaflet views of St Paul's and Westminster, the Thames at Windsor and a cross-Channel packet surround their stirring promises.

At about the same time, the Zealand Steamship Co. in collaboration with the Netherlands State Railway Co. offered a colourful little bookmark, over-printed on the verso with the name and address of John and E. Bumpus Ltd, Booksellers to the Queen. The bookmark advertises 'Fast train Services between England and the Continent via Flushing. The Quickest Route between Holland and Germany, Austria etc via Emmerich'. These fragments of ephemera can serve as a bridge for what can be found when travelling today. I have taken two short European holidays — because the material is to hand — one was a weekend visit to Holland in 1973 and the other a two week holiday in Italy the year before.

Our weekend trip to Holland was to visit an exhibition of English Delft pottery at the Rijksmuseum in Amsterdam. The Italian holiday was mainly to look at Italian paintings in Venice and Tuscany. These somewhat cultural activities were comfortably counterbalanced by food and drink. The background picture to the visit, quite apart from the innumerable catalogues and postcard reproductions of paintings, and other museum objects was made up of train, boat and air tickets and time-tables, baggage labels and receipts for food and drink, sugar packets, beer mats and drink labels, food wrappers and hotel letterheads, a 'NON DISTURBARE' notice and hotel bills. The words in these pieces of print are often of more interest than the visual impact of the bill or notice, however exciting they may be, and some of them are very exciting. The Bols label has plenty of typographic punch about it and looks well on its stoneware bottle. The Bokma label for another Dutch gin is less effective, but does recall the smoothness of that old Friesian Genever.

For that short visit to Holland we travelled by the Zeeland Steamship Company's day boat, the *Koningen Juliana*, and, as the bill reminds us, lunched off smoked eel and roast chicken, drinking beer and Bols. We stayed a night at the *Bad Hotel* at Scheveningen and collected a bill and a gift packet of shoe-shine. We took a train to Amsterdam for our visit to the Rijksmuseum. The next night we were at Zierickzee in Zeeland and apparently fed off lobster soup

c. 1830 Stage coach notice.
175×112 mm.

LONDON AND PARIS COACHES.

THE UNION
SAFE COACHES,
FROM THE
UNION AND ANTWERP HOTELS,
Gun and Castle Inns,
AND
45, SNARGATE STREET,
DOVER,
Every Morning at 8 and IO o'clock, and Evening at 6;
TO THE
White Bear, Piccadilly;
BLOSSOMS' INN, LAWRENCE LANE,
Cheapside;
BELL AND CROWN, HOLBORN;
AND **II,**
Gracechurch Street, London;
From whence they return every Morning at half-past 7,
and II o'clock; and Evening at 7.

From Dover to London without changing Coaches
or Coachmen.
Chitty, Back, Gilbert, Sanders, and Co. *Proprietors.*

and grilled soles. During the day to keep up our strength, we bought a box of Hopjes, which are coffee-flavoured caramels, and a delicious honey cake with a most decorative wrapper and a packet of syrupwafels. No doubt every traveller will have different tastes and could bring back quite different ephemeral printing.

Looking back at some of the stuff we have collected on our visits abroad, people might think we spent all our time poking about in museums and art galleries or eating and drinking. This is, I hope, a somewhat false picture! However, the sight of an old wine label or the receipt for a good meal can bring back comforting memories. And there is more to these bits of paper than that. The detailed bill from the *Hotel Villa Cipriani* at Asolo, though dull enough to look at, will, with current inflation, make interesting reading in a few years' time.

REDUCED FARES!!!

MESSAGERIES ROYALES,
Rue Notre Dame des Victoires, à Paris.

NEW ENGLISH DILIGENCES TO PARIS,

Every Morning and Evening at Six o'Clock,
FROM
THE WHITE BEAR, PICCADILLY, LONDON,
Also from the Cross Keys, Wood Street, Cheapside,
THE only Offices in London corresponding with the above *Company*, and where
Places can be secured to

PARIS, DOVER, CALAIS,

AMIENS,	OSTEND,	TOURS,	GENEVA,	BAYONNE,
ABBEVILLE,	CAMBRAY,	TOULOUSE,	MOULINS,	TURIN,
BRUSSELS,	VALENCIENNE,	LYON,	STRASBOURG,	MILAN,
LILLE,	BORDEAUX,	DIJON,	MARSEILLE,	&c. &c.

Packet-boats are always ready, at *Dover*, for the conveyance of Passengers booked throughout; but persons wishing to stop on the road, are allowed to do it, and resume their journey at
pleasure, without any extra expence, provided it is mentioned when the place is taken.

A NEW ENGLISH LIGHT COACH leaves Calais every Morning at 10 o'clock, through *Boulogne,
Montreuil, Abbéville, Amiens,* &c. and performs the journey in *thirty-six hours.* The Fares by this
Coach are:

From London to Paris {Inside .... 3*l.* 14*s.* 0*d.*} *Passage by Sea included.*
{Cabriolet ...... 3*l.* 2*s.* 0*d.*}
{Outside......... 2*l.* 14*s.* 0*d.*}

Another ENGLISH LIGHT COACH leaves CALAIS every Afternoon at 5 o'clock, through *Boulogne,
Montreuil, Abbeville, Poix, Beauvais,* &c. and arrives at PARIS in 30 *hours.* The Fares are as
follows:

From London to Paris {Inside ....3*l.* 14*s.* 0*d.*} *Passage by Sea included.*
{Cabriolet......3*l.* 2*s.* 0*d.*}

At Calais, apply to Mr. *Tarnier,* Director, at the Coach Office, *Messe-Meurice's Hotel,* Rue de
Prison, from whence Coaches set out every Day for the places above mentioned.

The Coach puts up at the *Paris Hotel,* Dover, kept by *Victor Poidevin,* and also at the *Ship Inn.*

There are also Coaches, three times a day, from the *White Bear* to
DOVER, RAMSGATE, MARGATE, DEAL, CANTERBURY, CHATHAM, ROCHESTER, AND GRAVESEND.

NOTICE.—*Persons sending Parcels to the Continent are requested to annex a written
Declaration of the contents and value; also the name and direction of the Person who sent it.*

. A Waggon to Dover three times a Week.

☞ *The Public are respectfully cautioned against the misrepresentations at the Black
Bear, and their pretending to Book through to Paris, for which they have no authority; the
Royal Messageries having no other Offices, in London, than the* WHITE BEAR, *Piccadilly,
and the* Cross Keys, *Wood Street, Cheapside.*

c. 1800–40 Continental hotel cards. Engraved, lithographed and printed by letterpress.
219×210 mm.

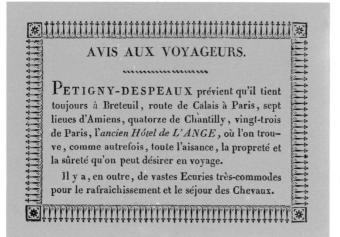

AVIS AUX VOYAGEURS.

PETIGNY-DESPEAUX prévient qu'il tient toujours à Breteuil, route de Calais à Paris, sept lieues d'Amiens, quatorze de Chantilly, vingt-trois de Paris, l'ancien Hôtel de L'ANGE, où l'on trouve, comme autrefois, toute l'aisance, la propreté et la sûreté qu'on peut désirer en voyage.

Il y a, en outre, de vastes Ecuries très-commodes pour le rafraîchissement et le séjour des Chevaux.

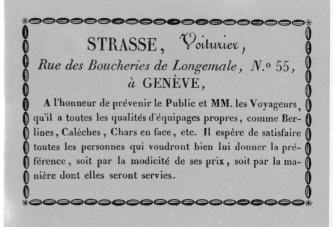

STRASSE, *Voiturier*, Rue des Boucheries de Longemale, N.º 55, à GENÈVE,

A l'honneur de prévenir le Public et MM. les Voyageurs, qu'il a toutes les qualités d'équipages propres, comme Berlines, Calèches, Chars en face, etc. Il espère de satisfaire toutes les personnes qui voudront bien lui donner la préférence, soit par la modicité de ses prix, soit par la manière dont elles seront servies.

LOGEMENT d. TOELAST.
Wed.º Beelenkamp, te Haarlem.
tegen over de Paardenpostery. Wyk 1 N.º 269.

HOTEL DU TOULAST.	TOOLAST HOTEL.
Veuve Beelenkamp	Widow Beelenkamp
à Haarlem. N.º 269.	at Haarlem.
vis a vis de la Poste aux chevaux	over a gainst the Posthouse.

HOTEL DU RHIN
près de la poste aux lettres, du bureau des omnibus pour le chemin de fer et des bateaux à vapeur.

Propriétaire : Fr. Schlund à BADEN-BADEN.

Table d'hôte à 1 et à 5 heures. — Restaurant toute la journée.

Recommandé par

C. H. Schrenke Gastgeber ZUR KAISER-WORTH am Markt zu GOSLAR.

Johan Reitz emphiehlt seinen Gasthof zum goldnen Kreuz in München Jean Reitz recommande son Hôtel à la Croix d'or à MUNIC.

c. 1840 Hotel letterhead.
85×170 mm.

c. 1840 Hotel card, lithographed by Kehr & Niessen Brothers
Cologne.
102×123 mm.

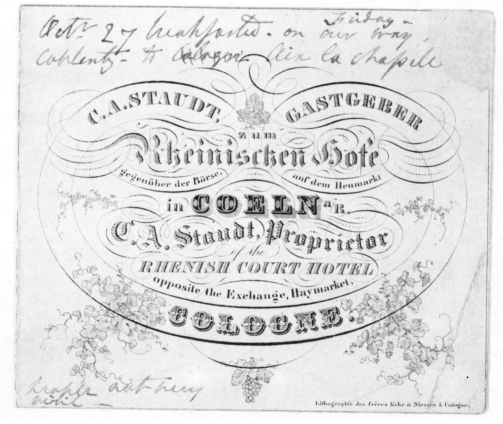

c. 1840 Hotel card engraved by Berndt and lithographed by
J. Trentsensky.
128×124 mm.

1839–79 French billheads, engraved, lithographed and printed by
letterpress.
285×200 mm.

c. 1860 Hotel card from Sestri du Levant.
85×127 mm.

À LA CORBEILLE DE FLEURS
19, Rue du Faub.ᵍ St. Honoré.

CHARDIN HOUBIGANT

Parfumeur

De L.L. A.A. R.R. Mademoiselle et M.ᵉˡˡᵉ d'Orléans.

Fabrique et tient Magasin de Parfumerie, Gants, Rouge Végétal, Sultans, Éventails et Objets de Goût. (N.ᵗᵃ Cette Maison n'a aucun dépôt dans Paris.)

Paris le _____ 18__

SPÉCIALITÉ DE BLANC DE FIL ET DE COTON
Location de Bâches pour Abris provisoires
ET BATTAGE DE GRAINS.
Confection sur Mesure de Chemises, Caleçons
et Gilets de flanelle.

DÉPÔT
de Toiles et Bâches Histasapes
et de Toiles transparentes
Pour Plans & Dessins
de C. Husson (Breveté).

DÉPÔT
de Couvertures de Laine
et de Coton
Fabrique de Devants de Chemises
en Percale
et en Toile Plis à la main

TOILES
Écrues, Jaunes, Blanches,
Grises, Vertes et Bleues,
Mouchoirs, Batistes
Linge de table uni et damassé,
Coutils et Toiles
à Matelas.

TOILES
de Coton, Blanches et Écrues,
Madapolams, Percales,
Jaconas, Nansouks
Mousselines unies brochées
et brodées, Broderies et
Dentelles, Cravates

BOSSON-HAVARD

Rue du Bercail, 3,
A ALENÇON.

TROUSSEAUX   **LAYETTES**

Mademoiselle Letouilleur   Doit

Payable comptant sans escompte de 5 p⁰⁄₀

Alençon le 3 Mai 1875

Valenciennes gothique   30   45

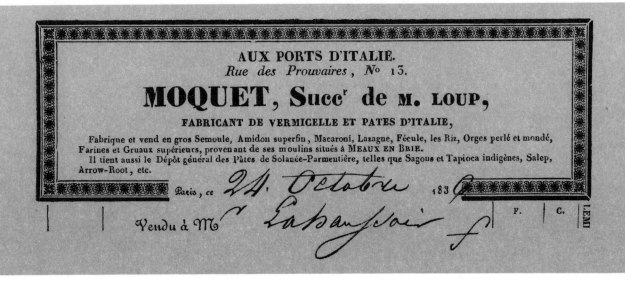

AUX PORTS D'ITALIE.
Rue des Prouvaires, N° 13.

MOQUET, Succᵣ de M. LOUP,

FABRICANT DE VERMICELLE ET PATES D'ITALIE,

Fabrique et vend en gros Semoule, Amidon superfin, Macaroni, Lazagne, Fécule, les Riz, Orges perlé et mondé, Farines et Gruaux supérieurs, provenant de ses moulins situés à MEAUX EN BRIE.
Il tient aussi le Dépôt général des Pâtes de Solanée-Parmentière, telles que Sagous et Tapioca indigènes, Salep, Arrow-Root, etc.

Paris, ce 24 Octobre 183

Vendu à Mᵣ

1973 Ephemera collected on a journey from Harwich to Amsterdam.
237×183 mm.

STOOMVAART
MAATSCHAPPIJ
ZEELAND

Hoek van Holland - Harwich

nota/bill   DATUM

M.S.

BEDIENDE

hoek van holland
harwich

COMPAGNIE INTERNATIONALE DES WAGONS-LITS
Aperitief of Jus de Fruits Gld 0.85
15 % bedieningsgeld niet inbegrepen
Dit reçu moet worden afgescheurd   C
in tegenwoordigheid van de reiziger
Roelants - Schiedam   Z.O.Z. 39423

COMPAGNIE INTERNATIONALE DES WAGONS-LITS
KOFFIE   -   Gld 0.34
OF NESCAFÉ
15 % bedieningsgeld niet inbegrepen
Dit reçu moet worden afgescheurd   CC
in tegenwoordigheid van de reiziger
Roelants - Schiedam   Z.O.Z. 61042

№ 2063

BEDIENING INBEGREPEN/GRATUITIES
Mocht U speciale wensen of klachten heb
Chef Steward

For special wishes or any complaint pleas

60

1973 Ephemera collected on same journey.
237×183 mm.

A 0 7 5 2
HOEK v HOLLAND
AMSTERDAM CS
1. kl.
PRIJS   Z.O.Z.

PRIJS   Z.O.Z.
HOEK v HOLLAND
AMSTERDAM CS
1. kl.
32551   0042

CRYSTAL LEERDAM
MADE IN HOLLAND

22. 05. 73

Uitsluitend
geldig op de
aangegeven dag
217 NS

- 13.60 085

Hero
Aardbeienjam
Extra
Inh. 35 gram

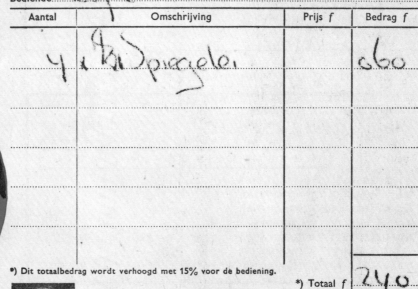

Cⁱᵉ INTˡᵉ DES WAGONS-LITS
et des Grands Express Européens
Kantoor etage Kamer 44
Centraal Station, AMSTERDAM

NEDERLAND
Klachten te richten aan nevenstaand
adres onder bijvoeging der nota.

Buffetdienst of Buffet-Restaurantdienst No. .... Datum ....
Treinstel No. ....   Trein No. ....
Bediende ....

Aantal	Omschrijving	Prijs *f*	Bedrag *f*
4	Spiegelei		060

*) Dit totaalbedrag wordt verhoogd met 15% voor de bediening.

*) Totaal *f* 240

ZHB *bier om in te bijten!*

Deze rekening moet in tegenwoordigheid van de reiziger
worden geschreven.

1973 Beermat, food and drink wrappers and label and billhead.
237 × 200 mm.

echt

GO

RESTAURANT - TAVERNE
HAVENPLEIN 7 - ZIERIKZEE
Telefoon 01110 - 2584
b.g.g. 2526

poorthuys

TAFEL No. 3

2 Stol	2 —
3 Oude Klaw	2 85
1 Crème d'asperges	1 ⁴⁵
1 Bisque d'homard	2 50
Sole Poorthuys	20 =

01285 *Service 15%* Tel. - sig. | 2 9 | 10 |
| | 4 38 |
TOTAAL | 3 3 45 |

19......

V.O. GENEVER GIN

Daar de gevestigde goede naam van ons huis gerigt
omstreeks den jare 1575, tot onedele concurrentie aanmaak
aanleiding heeft gegeven en wij dit misbruik zoo veel mogelijk
wenschen tegen te gaan, zoo voegen wij van a
flesschen en kruiken waarop ons fabrikaat is
en behalve ons bekende Merk FABRIEK 'T LOOTSJE
etikette met onze handteekening

66° PROOF

Lucas Bols

en z aar aanleiding der bestaande Internationale
Wetten onen gestreng vervolgen die ons Merk namaken
of verv en. AMSTERDAM den 1 Januarij 1868.

DISTILLED IN HOLLAND.

1973 Food wrapper, beermat, museum ticket and catalogue cover.
237 × 200 mm.

1973 Hotel billhead and label, complimentary shoeshine pack and Inter-City timetable.
237×183 mm.

1973 Dutch food and drink wrappers and labels.
361×211 mm.

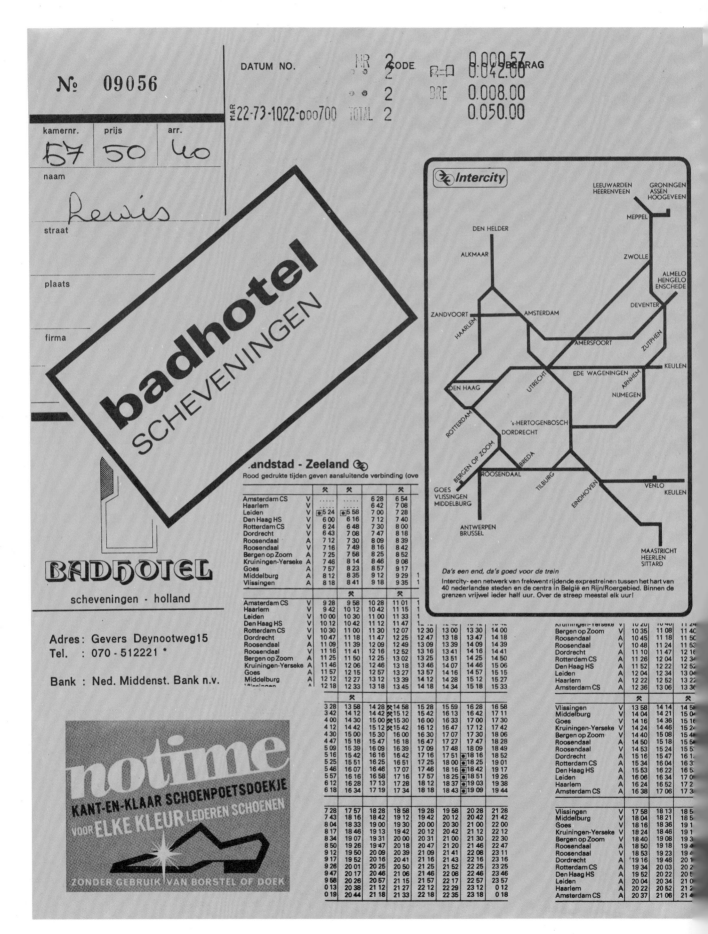

1972 Italian food wrappers and labels.
268×211 mm.

1972 Hotel bill.
210×165 mm.

HOTEL
VILLA CIPRIANI
ASOLO

TELEF. 52.166 - 52.298

APPARTAMENTO

N. 306

N° 2984

HOTEL CIPRIANI
TELEF. 85.068   VENEZIA

HARRY'S BAR
TELEF. 85.331   VENEZIA

LOCANDA CIPRIANI
TELEF. 730.150   TORCELLO

Sig. Mora Lewis

A B D

Arrangiamento: Appartamento

Pensione

Spiegazione dei Riferimenti			Riga	Data	Numero progr.	Numero camera	Importo	Riferimento
APP	Appartamento	- Apartment	1	11 IX	5990	306	* 11880	PEN
PEN	Pensione	- Pension	2	11 IX	5991	306	* 00120	SOG
RIS	Ristorante	- Restaurant	3	11 IX	5992	306	* 00500	CAN
CAN	Cantina	- Drinks	4	11 IX	5993	306	* 00200	CAF
CAF	Caffetteria	- Breakfast - Coffee, tea	5	11 IX	5994	306	* 00300	BAR
BAR	Bar	- Bar	6	11 IX	5995	000	* 13000	To
TEL	Telefono	- Telephone	7	12 IX	6428	306	* 11880	PEN
BIA	Biancheria	- Laundry or pressing	8	12 IX	6429	306	* 00120	SOG
DIV	Diversi	- Sundries	9	12 IX	6430	306	* 00400	CAN
%	Servizio	- Service	10	12 IX	6431	000	* 25400	To
IGE	I. G. E.	- Gvt. Tax	11	13 IX	6825	306	* 11880	PEN
SOG	Soggiorno	- Town Tax	12	13 IX	6826	306	* 00120	SOG
BOL	Bollo	- Revenue stamp	13	13 IX	6827	306	* 00700	CAN
CAS	Cassa	- Cash paid	14	13 IX	6828	306	* 00200	CAF
SCO	Sconto	- Discount	15	13 IX	6829	000	* 00500	CAF
CC	Correzione a credito	Corrections	16	13 IX	6830	000	* 38800	To
CD	Correzione a debito		17	14 IX	7003	306	* 00100	BOL
			18	14 IX	7004	000	* 38900	To

FONTESTAMPA - TEL 57.463

SI PREGA DI VOLER SALDARE
I CONTI ALLA PRESENTAZIONE

Il Cassiere

IGE PAGATA IN ABBONAMENTO

1972 Italian museum and canal tickets.
237×183 mm.

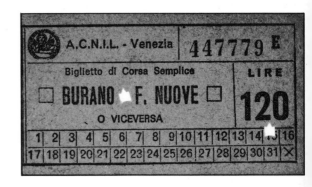

1972 Italian museum tickets.
237×183 mm.

COMUNE DI VENEZIA

**INGRESSO AL
CIVICO MUSEO
CORRER**

L. 100

Serie R   № 008465

GE corrisposta in modo virtuale
ut. Min. 84690 del 18 - 2 - 1953

COMUNE
DI VERONA

**INGRESSO
MUSEO
CASTELVECCHIO**

№ **15006**

1 2 3 4 5 6 7 8 9 10 11 12 13 14 15 16 17 18 19 20 21 22 23 24 25 26 27 28 29 30 31

CASTELLO DI MALCESINE

Biglietto d'ingresso
al CASTELLO e al MUSEO

L. 150   № 65487

L'Imposta sulla Entrata dovuta sul presente biglietto viene corrisposta in modo virtuale all'Ufficio del Registro di Caprino Veronese, giusta autorizzazione ministeriale n. 161417 del 20 - 7 - 1963.

Conservare il biglietto per eventuali controlli

BIGLIETTO VALEVOLE PER UNA PERSONA

VILLA DI MASER

ISITA AL CICLO DEGLI AFFRESCHI DI PAOLO VERONESE

LA BIENNALE DI VENEZIA
6ª ESPOSIZIONE INTERNAZIONALE D'ARTE
11 GIUGNO - 1º OTTOBRE 1972

INGRESSO ALLA MOSTRA

CAPOLAVORI PITTURA 20º SECOLO

MUSEO CORRER, PIAZZA S. MARCO

L. 300

13981

BIMOSPA-ROMA

№ 53488

BASILICA
DI
S. MARIA
GLORIOSA
DEI FRARI

1972 Hotel letterhead, label and sign. BEA baggage tag.
237×184 mm.

4. Changes in Transport

The roads everywhere in the eighteenth century were in a very poor condition. Coaches and carriages were often overturned because of this. The *Encyclopedia Britannica* describes how 'the turnpike roads were generally managed by ignorant and incompetent men until Telford and Mc-Adam brought scientific principles and regular system to their construction and repair'.

The stage coach as a method of public transport was in use in England in the sixteenth century. By the end of the eighteenth century, stage coaches, usually drawn by four horses, ran on regular routes to all parts of Britain. From 1784 English coaches began to carry the mail. Soon after this mail coaches were running on the Continent and in America. By 1835 there were over 700 mail coaches running throughout Britain. The term 'diligence' referred to on page 55 in the '*Messageries Royales*' bill, was merely another name for a similar four-wheeled coach.

In spite of the exuberant ease shown by drivers of the US Mail in Westerns, driving a team of four horses needed much skill. Driving a coach-and-four soon became a sport for amateurs. Various clubs were started, including, in England the Four-in-hand Club (1856) and in the USA the New York Coaching Club (1875).

Charles Dickens gives a graphic description of the pleasures to be had when riding outside on a stage coach, when he describes the visit of the Pickwick Club to Dingley Dell. 'The guard and Mr Weller disappear for five minutes, most probably to get the hot brandy and water, for they smell very strongly of it, when they return, the coachman mounts to the box, Mr Weller jumps up behind, the Pickwickians pull their coats round their legs, and their shawls over their noses; the helpers pull the horse-cloths off, the coachman shouts out a cheery "All right," and away they go.

'They have rumbled through the streets, and jolted over the stones, and at length reach the wide and open country. The wheels skim over the hard and frosty ground; and the horses bursting into a canter at a smart crack of the whip, step along the road as if the load behind them, coach, passengers, cod-fish, oyster barrels and all, were but a feather at their heels. They have descended a gentle slope, and enter upon a level, as compact and dry as a solid block of marble, two miles long. Another crack of the whip, and on they speed, at a smart gallop, the horses tossing their heads and rattling the harness as if in exhilaration at the rapidity of the motion, while the coachman, holding whip and reins in one hand, takes off his hat with the other, and resting it on his knees, pulls out his handkerchief, and wipes his forehead, partly because he has a habit of doing it, and partly because it's as well to shew the passengers how cool he is, and what an easy thing it is to drive a four-in-hand, when you have had as much practice as he has ... they pull up at the inn yard, where the fresh horses, with cloths on, are already waiting. The coachman throws down the reins and gets down himself, and the other outside passengers drop down also, except those who have no great confidence in their ability to get up again, and they remain where they are, and stamp their feet against the coach to warm them; looking with longing eyes and red noses at the bright fire in the inn bar, and the sprigs of holly with red berries which ornament the window.'

The woodcut at the bottom of the page is one of a series of printer's stock blocks issued by an unidentified English printer in the 1820s. This one cost 42 shillings. The additional blocks (over the page) from the same printer show a heavy covered waggon, drawn by a team of eight horses and a fly-van. The term 'fly' was usually used for a one-horse hackney carriage, but here presumably meant a light, fast vehicle which was drawn by four horses.

In 1820 the New York–Philadelphia coach used to leave Battery Point aboard the steam boat *Nautilus*, and travelling via Staten Island, New Brunswick, Princeton and Trenton would arrive at Philadelphia at 6.0 p.m., a journey of eleven and a half hours, for a fare of $5. Another travel bill in the Bella C. Landauer collection shows the Mail Stage Coach from Boston to Albany taking two days in

c. 1815 Stock block.
270 × 150 mm.

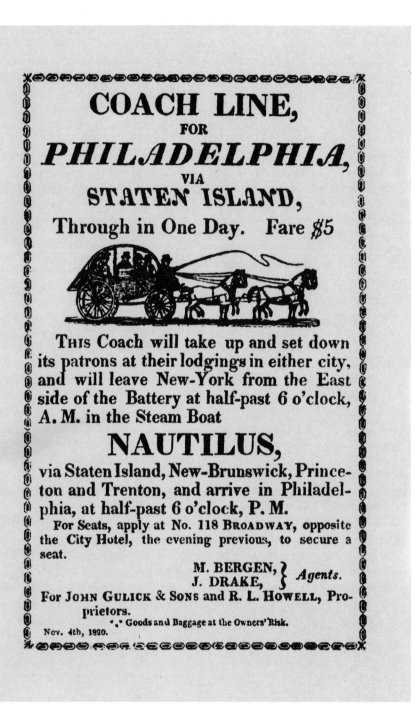

1830 for the journey, for a fare of $6. The woodcuts for the coaches on both these bills are almost identical.

Though passenger railway services were in use by 1840, stage coaches continued to run on certain routes for the next half century. For short journeys and for private transport, horse-drawn waggons, cabs and carriages continued in use until after the First World War. Every town had its curriers, saddlers and harness manufacturers. Large places also had their carriage works, such as the Old Swinford Carriage Works at Stourbridge. The letterhead for this firm on pages 72–73, is printed on a vivid pink paper and has twenty different carriage designs illustrated on the back.

Licences, certificates, etc provide an area of printed ephemera that can illustrate many other things beside transport. The Inland Revenue, that cross we all have to bear, was already in business in England in the nineteenth century, taxing horse-drawn transportation. In 1872 the licence in England for a carriage cost £2.2.0 and for a horse or mule 10s 6d. These particular licences were issued at Grasmere in Westmoreland.

This brings us to the modern Road Fund licence, road taxes and the motor car and omnibus. Their story can be

illustrated in a hundred different ways, with the use of licences, billheads, bus tickets, printers' stock blocks and cigarette cards.

The coach and bus tickets issued by London Transport shown here, though only twenty or so years old, are a part of transport history. They have been superseded by miserable little strips of stamped paper, punched out of the conductor's ticket machine.

The char-à-banc and the solid-wheeled lorry are cuts from a typefounder, the Peugeot and Swift card were issued respectively by Brooke Bond Tea in the 1960s and by Lambert and Butler with their cigarettes in the 1920s. This is but a tasting. The possibilities of illustrating old or modern road transport by contemporary printed ephemera are infinite.

Telephone Nos. { High Street, West Bromwich, 30X.
{ Great Bridge,   ,,   24X.

West Bromwich, Great Bridge & Hill Top,

Dec 13th   19

Mr Stanley

Dr. to

C. & S. BAGGOTT, Ltd.,

(Late COLEMAN)

Curriers, Saddlers, Collar and Harness Manufacturers.

LEATHER MACHINE BAND MANUFACTURERS.

PATENT LEATHER LEGGINGS, HORSE CLOTHING, RUGS, WHIPS, &c., TO ORDER.

1 x 7 lb Boat Line	*4*	*11*
Pd to E Drepa		
for C & S. Baggett Ld		

TELEGRAMS:-
"BEDDOES MOORE":
"STOURBRIDGE":
TELEPHONE 34.

OLDSWINFORD CARRIAGE WORKS,

CARRIAGE EXPERT
AND
VALUER FOR "BAZAAR,
EXCHANGE & MART."

Stourbridge,   *Mch 31*   *1903*

To W. B. Moore,

Carriage Manufacturer,

POST NUBILA PHŒBUS

J & C COOPER, LONDON, COPYRIGHT

Carriages of every description made to order & old ones taken in Exchange.

HORSES, CARRIAGES &c LET ON HIRE BY THE DAY WEEK MONTH OR FOR A LONGER PERIOD

		3

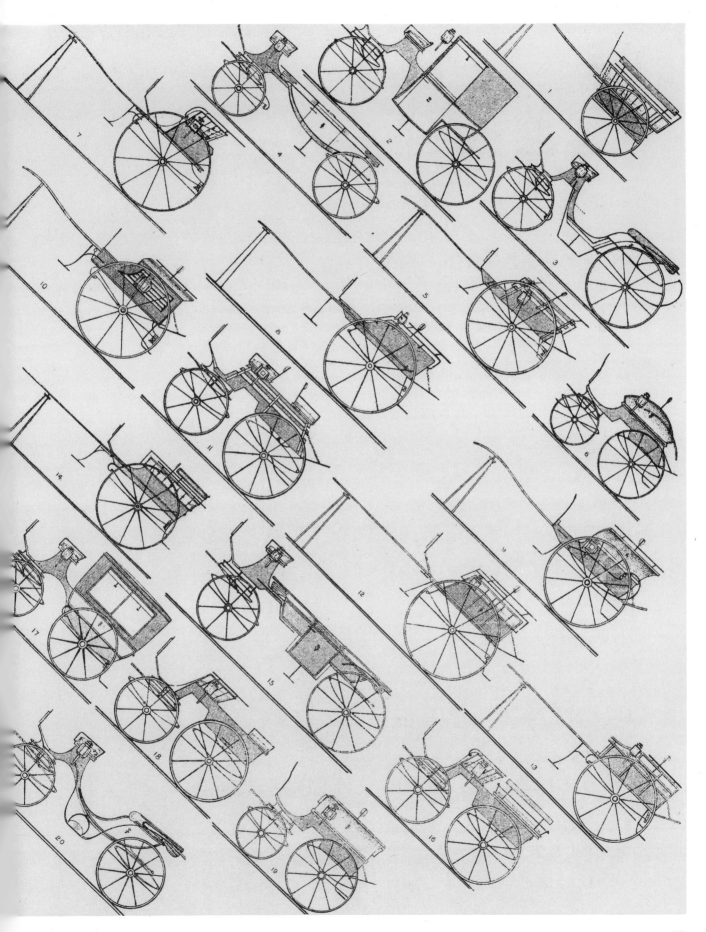

1872 Licence for carriage.
155×143 mm.

1972 Verso of Carriage Museum ticket.
90×202 mm.

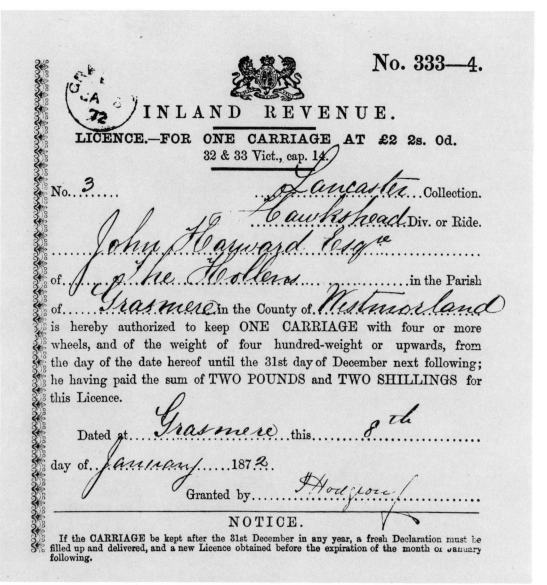

No. 333—4.

INLAND REVENUE.

LICENCE.—FOR ONE CARRIAGE AT £2 2s. 0d.
32 & 33 Vict., cap. 14.

No. *3* ....*Lancaster*...Collection.
.............................*Hawkshead*.Div. or Ride.

.............*John Hayward Esqre*.......................

of.......*The Hollens*...................in the Parish

of.......*Grasmere*.in the County of.....*Westmorland*

is hereby authorized to keep ONE CARRIAGE with four or more
wheels, and of the weight of four hundred-weight or upwards, from
the day of the date hereof until the 31st day of December next following;
he having paid the sum of TWO POUNDS and TWO SHILLINGS for
this Licence.

Dated at.......*Grasmere*...this........*8th*.............

day of..*January*.....187*2*.

Granted by......*Hodgson*.................

NOTICE.

If the CARRIAGE be kept after the 31st December in any year, a fresh Declaration must be
filled up and delivered, and a new Licence obtained before the expiration of the month of January
following.

*MUSEO DELLE
CARROZZE
DELLA VILLA
DI MASER*

74

1872 Licence for horse or mule.
155×143 mm.

1870 Stock block from Bewick's workshop.
80×145 mm.

No. 333—1.

INLAND REVENUE.

LICENCE.—FOR ONE HORSE OR MULE £0 10s. 6d.
32 & 33 Vict., cap. 14.

No..*7*..... ....*Lancaster*......Collection.

....*Hawkshead*..Div. or Ride.

..........*John Harward Esq*...........

of.....*The Hollins*.... ....in the Parish

of...*Grasmere*....in the County of.....*Westmorland*....

is hereby authorized to keep ONE HORSE or MULE from the day of the
date hereof until the 31st day of December next following; he having paid
the sum of TEN SHILLINGS and SIXPENCE for this Licence.

Dated at....*Grasmere*....this....*8*....

day of..*January*.....187*2*..

Granted by..*Hodgson*..............

NOTICE.

If the HORSE or MULE be kept after the 31st December in any year, a fresh Declaration must be filled up and delivered, and a new Licence obtained before the expiration of the month of January following.

1906–1959 Motoring ephemera. Garage billhead, stock blocks,
trade and cigarette cards, vehicle licence, sugar wrappers.
234×183 mm.

The 'Railway Age' took hold of people's imaginations just as the Space Age does today – perhaps more so, because it was closer to them. People rushed to buy shares in newly formed companies. Fortunes were made and lost.

The Stockton and Darlington Public Railway was the first public railway opened for passengers and goods traffic anywhere in the world. To begin with the coaches and trucks were horse drawn apart from a single loco-motive, appropriately named *Locomotion*. It was built by George Stephenson. In 1828 the Delaware and Hudson Canal Company hearing of the success of the Stockton and Darlington Railway ordered four locomotives from England. The first one of these, named *America*, arrived in the United States in January 1829. It was designed and built by Stephenson. The other three engines were built by Foster & Rastrick at Stourbridge and arrived soon after. One of these the *Stourbridge Lion* was actually the first

locomotive to run upon rails in America, being driven along a section of the Delaware and Hudson Canal Company's railroad in August 1829.

The railway story I have to tell here, fairly typical of such histories in Britain and America, begins with a bill announcing a public meeting concerning a plan for a new railroad, which was to become known as the Birmingham and Gloucester Railway. A scheme for this railway had been put up by various Bristol businessmen in 1824. In 1832 Isambard Kingdom Brunel surveyed the route for this proposed railroad. He chose an open country route (with an awkward incline) to avoid towns such as Stour-bridge and Dudley, and the cost of buying land in those well-to-do places. In spite of the meeting at Kidderminster, lack of capital held back progress and it was not until 1840 that the first section was opened and a year later before the line was completed. The Lickey incline proved so severe that the Birmingham and Gloucester directors felt that there was no English locomotive strong enough to haul their trains up its 1 in 37 gradient. So they ordered eight engines from Norris and Co of Philadelphia. The first to arrive was named after that city. It was twelve years from the time the Delaware and Hudson Canal Company had bought their locomotives from England. Now the com-pliment was returned. In 1846, the Birmingham and Gloucester Railway was taken over by the Midland Railway.

The story can be taken a stage further, with a billhead from G. J. Eveson, Coal, Coke, Lime, Limestone, Iron, Iron Ore & Paint Ore Merchant, and another billhead from Caleb Lewis, Wholesale Potato Merchant. Both these merchants have spirited engravings of locomotives and trains. Mr Eveson's train is drawn by no known make of locomotive, but the other is more accurate. In using printed ephemera for more serious purposes, it may be advisable to use backing-up material to confirm a point or illustrate more accurately some particular intent or object. Photostats of drawings of locomotives from Clement E. Stretton's *The Development of the Locomotive 1863–1903* are used here to correct the inaccuracies in the illustrations on such letterheads as these. Caleb Lewis's engine is a fairly free rendering of Matthew Kirtley's Express Engine, built for the Midland Railway Company in 1864–65. These engines, with 6 foot 8 inch driving wheels (2 metres 03), were remarkable for the heavy work which they per-formed and for their economy in both fuel and main-tenance.

In the nineteenth century the American locomotives soon outstripped the English ones in size and in power. The Pennsylvania Railroad had some absolutely gigantic engines for hauling their very heavy trains up the gradients between New York, Philadelphia and Pittsburg. The most distinctive features of many of the American engines (such as those illustrated on page 81) were the massive smoke stacks used by all wood-burning engines and the 'cow-catchers' in front.

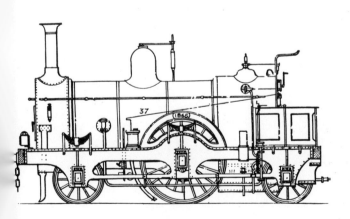

840 *Philadelphia*: Birmingham and Gloucester Railway locomotive, built by Norris and Co. of Philadelphia.

864 Kirtley's Express engine, Midland Railway Company. From *he Development of the Locomotive 1803–1903* by .. E. Stretton. Crosby Lockwood. 1903.

Public Meeting

RESPECTING

GLOUCESTER, WORCESTER,

Kidderminster, Stourbridge, Dudley,

AND

BIRMINGHAM

RAILWAY.

TO THE

HIGH BAILIFF

OF THE BOROUGH OF

KIDDERMINSTER.

Sir,

WE, the undersigned, request that you will call an early MEETING of the Inhabitants of this Town, and any other PERSONS in this NEIGHBOURHOOD feeling interested, to take into consideration the Plan of a RAIL ROAD by Mr. Wooddeson, Civil Engineer, to communicate with the **LONDON RAIL ROAD** at **BIRMINGHAM;**—and **CAMBRIAN RAILWAY** at **GLOUCESTER ;**—the particulars of which will be explained by that Gentleman, who is now in this Town, and will attend such Meeting.

JOHN GOUGH, Jun.
PARDOE, HOOMAN, & PARDOE
J. MORTON
JOSEPH NEWCOMB
WATSON, SON, & BADLAND
G. & H. TALBOT & SONS
JOHN GOUGH & SONS
THOS. HALLEN.

In compliance with the above highly respectable Requisition, I hereby appoint a Meeting, for the purpose therein mentioned, to be held at the Guildhall, in the said Borough, on FRIDAY Next, the 22d inst. at Eleven o'Clock in the Forenoon.

S. BEDDOES,

Kidderminster, Nov. 19th, 1833.   *HIGH BAILIFF.*

THOMAS PENNELL, PRINTER, HIGH-STREET, KIDDERMINSTER.

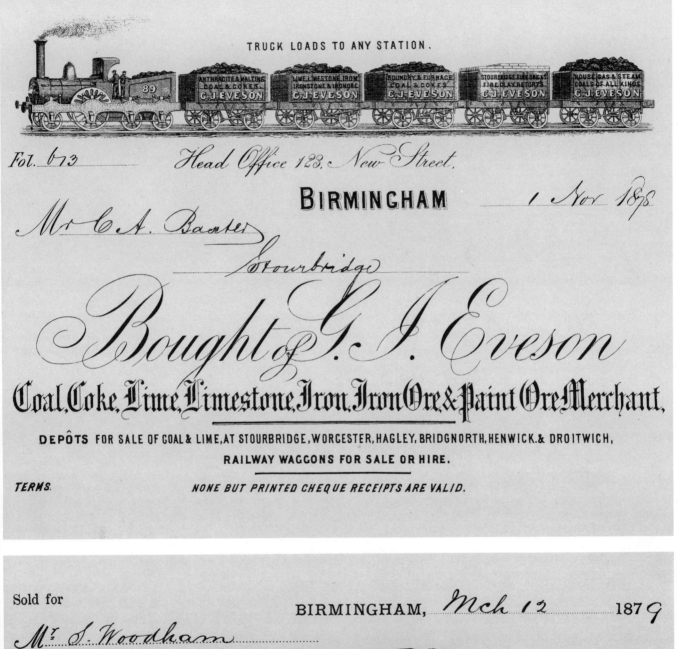

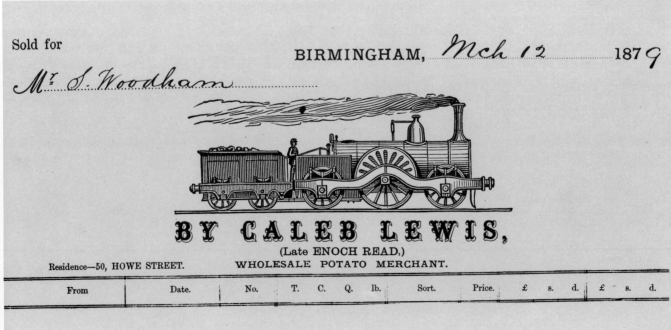

1873 Railway instruction notes.
245×182 mm and 103×165 mm.

1840–1925 Railway ephemera. Christmas card by William Fenton
of a Great Northern locomotive (1870). Stick-on baggage labels
(1920–25) and postcard of German toy train (c. 1840) *Bethnal
Green Museum.*

(517)—[Appendix to R. C. H. Goods Managers'
Meeting, 26th January, 1869, A.]

London and North Western Railway.

The London & North Western Railway Company give Public Notice that they hold themselves entirely relieved from loss of or damage done to all goods, matters, or things described in the Act of William IV., cap. 68, unless the particular articles be declared, and an assurance over and above the carriage be paid as compensation for the risk incurred.

That in respect of any animals, luggage, or goods booked through, and to be carried partly by railway and partly by sea, and partly by canal and partly by sea the Company shall be exempted from liability for any loss or damage which may arise during the carriage of any such animals, luggage, or goods, from the act of God, the king's enemies, fire, accidents from machinery, boilers, and steam, and all and every other dangers and accidents of the seas, rivers, and navigation of whatever nature and kind soever, in the same manner as if the Company had signed and delivered to the consignor a bill of lading containing such conditions.

That no claim for loss or damage for which they may be liable will be allowed, unless the same be made within Three days after delivery of the goods; such delivery to be considered complete when notice of arrival is sent to the consignee, or, if the goods be carted by the Company, when they are unloaded at the door of the consignee's place of abode or business.

That all goods conveyed—but which the Company have not undertaken to deliver—must be removed from the Company's trucks within Forty-eight hours after notice of arrival is sent to consignee, or they will, after the expiration of that time, be subject to an additional charge beyond the amount due for carriage thereof, of Three Shillings per truck per day or part of a day, for demurrage of such truck, and be held by the Company—not as common carriers, but as warehousemen—at owner's sole risk.

That they do not, except on special conditions, undertake the carriage of gunpowder, lucifer matches, aqua fortis, oil of vitriol, or other dangerous articles, neither will they, under any circumstances, be liable for the loss of any such article; but all senders thereof will be held accountable for any damage arising thereto or therefrom, and whether to other goods or property of the Company or of any other person. Senders are subject to a Penalty of Twenty Pounds, unless the nature of the contents be declared and distinctly marked on the outside of the package containing the same.

That all goods delivered to the Company will be received and held by them, subject to a general lien for money due to them, whether for carriage of such goods or for other charges; and in case the general lien is not satisfied within a reasonable time from the day when the Company first received the goods, the same will be sold by the company by auction or otherwise, and the proceeds of sale applied to the satisfaction of such lien and expenses.

Windermere STATION, *June 7* 187 3

ADVICE OF GOODS.

Mr W. Cole

The undermentioned Goods, consigned to you, having arrived at this Station, I will thank you for instructions as to their removal *Grassmere* either to remain here to your order, and are now held by the Company—not as common carriers, but as warehousemen—at owner's sole risk, and subject to the usual warehouse charges, in addition to the charges now advised.

When you send for the Goods, please to send this Note.

No delivery effected after *6* o'Clock in the Evening.

The Directors require the Carriage to be Paid on Delivery, unless the Consignee has a Ledger Account with the Company.

For the London and North Western Railway Company,

Signature, *Harlam*

McCorquodale & Co., Printers, London—Works, Newton.

INVOICE No.	FROM	DESCRIPTION OF GOODS.	MARKS.	WEIGHT. T. C. Q. lbs.	RATE. £ s. d.	PAID ON. £ s. d.	TOTAL TO PAY. £ s. d.
99	Waterloo	12 Sh. Corn		15 2 74			16 7
	Received June 9. 73		7 3				1
	pro.						16 8

(19a— 12/22.)

Form C.

(A supply of these Forms must be kept in each Signal Box.)

London & North Western Railway.

Authority for Driver to travel on the Wrong Line in case of Accident.

To Driver of Engine No._____ working_____ m. Train

From_____ to_____,_____

I authorise you to return with your Train on the *_____ line in the wrong direction to this Signal Box.

Signature of_____ Signalman.

at_____ Signal Box.

Date_____ 19__   Time issued_____ .m.

Catch Points exist at_____

[SEE OVER.

* *Insert name of line, for example, Main, Fast, Slow, or Goods.*

(²⁄₄₇) SOUTHERN RAILWAY. (Stock. 34H)

TO

L. & N. E. Rly.,

Via _____ and MARYLEBONE.

(¹¹⁄₅₈) SOUTHERN RAILWAY. (Stock. 34 V)

TO

L. & N. E. Rly.,

Via _____ and KING'S CROSS.

London and South Western Ry.
787
TO

Farnham

(¹²⁄₈₅) SOUTHERN RAILWAY.
(787 L.A.)
From WATERLOO
TO

COWES

Via PORTSMOUTH & RYDE.

1924–37 Railway cigarette cards issued by W.D. & H.O. Wills and
Gallahers Ltd.
Each card 36 × 67 mm.

ON THE FOOTPLATE OF A MODERN LOCOMOTIVE.

LOCOMOTIVE HEAD CODES

COLOUR LIGHT SIGNALS

"PACIFIC" EXPRESS LOCOMOTIVE "PAPYRUS," L.N.E.R.

"KING" CLASS EXPRESS LOCOMOTIVE "KING GEORGE V," G.W.R.

AUTOMATIC TRAIN CONTROL SYSTEM

L.M. & S.R. CALEDONIAN SECTION

L.M. & S.R. NORTH STAFFORDSHIRE SECTION.

STREAMLINED STEAM TRAIN
PARIS, LYONS & MEDITERRANEAN RLY.

STREAMLINED LOCOMOTIVE
CANADIAN NATIONAL RAILWAYS

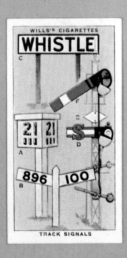

TRACK SIGNALS

ARTICULATED HEAVY FREIGHT LOCO., NORTHERN PACIFIC RAILWAY, U.S.A.

HEAVY PASSENGER AND FREIGHT LOCOMOTIVE, CANADIAN PACIFIC

opposite page

c. 1870. American locomotives on a Boston billhead and on stock
blocks from Mckellar, Smiths and Jordan Typefoundry,
Philadelphia.
247 × 220 mm.

1901 Timetable cover.
133 × 78 mm.

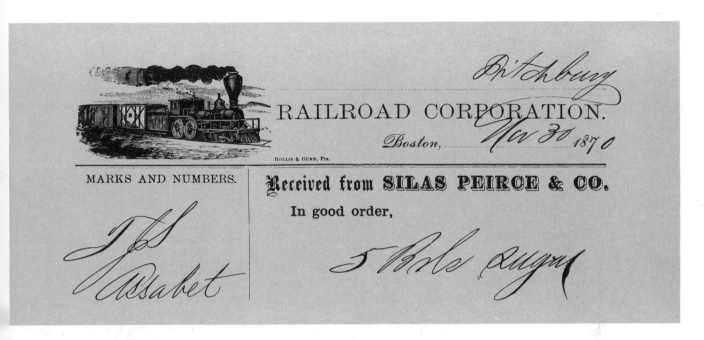

We have had resource to printers' stock blocks as an aid
to ephemeral illustration when looking at the early days of
road transport. The Railroad Corporation of Boston, Mass.
are clearly using a stock block on their letterhead. Whether
their printers Hollis and Gunn obtained it from the
Mackellar, Smiths and Jordan Typefoundry of Philadelphia
is not certain. This foundry carried a quantity of such cuts
(eight of these are illustrated here). The smaller ones are
actually cast to type sizes, 36pt and 30pt respectively.

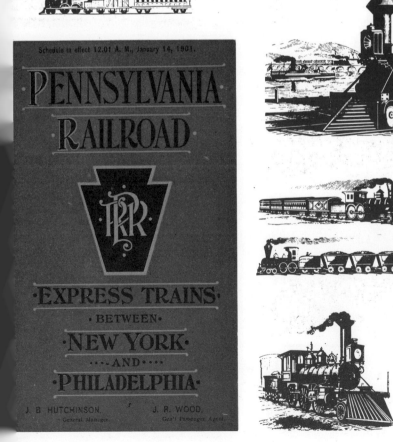

SPECIMENS OF LARGER RAILROAD CUTS FURNISHED TO ORDER.

Cigarette cards (or their modern equivalent, tea cards) are collectable objects in their own right. They are attractive things and there is the additional satisfaction of completing a set of such cards. They are also useful and informative pieces of ephemeral printing. Numerous sets of cards on railway subjects have been issued over the years. Of the cards in the colour plate opposite page 81, the three in the left-hand column and the two at the head of the other columns come from a series called *Railway Equipment*, issued by W.D. & H.O. Wills in 1939. The remainder are from a series called *Railway Engines*, issued by Wills in 1924, except for the two cards of streamlined locomotives for the Paris, Lyons and Mediterranean Railway and the Canadian National Railway. These come from a set called *Trains of the World*, issued by Gallaher in 1937.

Whereas this colour plate is thoroughly informative, the previous one is little more than decorative. At the head of the page is a Christmas card with a drawing by William Fenton of a Great Northern Express engine 4-2-2, designed by Patrick Stirling in 1870. Between the Southern Railway and London and South Western Railway baggage labels is a postcard from the Bethnal Green Museum, showing a very early clockwork toy engine with the name plate *Bavaria* on its side and with tender and carriage of painted tin plate. It was made about 1840 and stands in front of its original box.

A file of railway documents, forms, advice notes and invoices came to light recently when a West Country solicitor was clearing up his office. These pieces of paper are a revelation of the number of long forgotten railways that were operating in Britain in the nineteenth century; also of the eventualities covered by these documents. For instance, the London & North Western Railway in their Advice of Goods form (shown on page 80), issued from Windermere station in 1873, inform a certain Mr Cole that his goods 'are held by the Company — not as common carriers, but as warehousemen — at owner's sole risk'. And how was he going to get them to Grasmere? The same railway produced the 'Authority for Driver to travel on the Wrong Line in case of Accident'.

Amongst other idiosyncratic pieces of print was a Special Advice Note issued by the Great Northern Railway in respect of Carrying Gunpowder or other explosives, and another for an 'Indemnity to be signed by passengers who require to travel in Bath chairs in the Guard's Van'. Excursion notices covered every sort of activity: the Oxford, Worcester and Wolverhampton Railway in 1853 offered reduced fares for an outing to Blenheim from Evesham; the London Chatham and Dover Railway in 1871 had a notice for a special train for the Dover Regatta; the London,

Brighton and South Coast Railway advertised in 1873 a cheap visit to the Grand Aquarium at Brighton. The Great Western Railway in 1868 had an excursion train to London for the Epsom Races (12 shillings return from Shrewsbury) and in 1914 the Isle of Wight Central Railway offered cheap rates for a Theatre Train to Portsmouth.

There were also many advice notes of consignments of coal etc., including one issued by the Vale of Clwyd Railway in 1860, a Pig Iron Warrant for the Furness Railway Company to the Askham Iron Works, Way Bills for the Cleator and Workington Junction Railway in 1920, the Eastern Counties Railway in 1857, the Denbigh, Ruthin and Corwen Railway in 1865 and the Neath and Brecon Railway in 1910. There were notices for 'Revised Parcel Rates' from the Hundred of Manhood and Selsey Tramways Company, Enquiry Forms for Lost Luggage from the Highland Railway, an instruction for a special coach to run from Penrith to Keswick from the Cockermouth, Keswick and Penrith Railway, and a ticket form issued in the 1860s by the Potteries, Shrewsbury and North Wales Railway Company for 'Soldiers, Policemen on Duty and Shipwrecked Mariners'.

There were many other pieces of railway ephemera, but the above gives some idea of the growth and scope of this industry. During the nineteenth century the trains were running faster and faster. The locomotive *Great Western*, built in 1846, reached 78 miles per hour (126 k.p.h.) and used to do the Paddington–Didcot run of $53\frac{1}{2}$ miles (86 km.) in 47 minutes.

In 1895, a special express train ran from New York to Albany, a distance of 143 miles in 134 minutes. Soon speeds of 80 miles per hour (130 k.p.h.) were being regularly maintained.

By 1935 the London and North Eastern Railway Pacific locomotive *Papyrus* (illustrated among the cigarette cards opposite page 81) broke the world speed record at 108 miles per hour (173 k.p.h.). She had at that time run 392,853 miles (632,221 km.). Even so in ninety years the rail speed had increased by less than fifty per cent.

One fast train that came to grief was the North British Dundee express, which on the night of 28 December 1879, whilst a great gale was blowing, plunged into the River Tay as the central section of the viaduct collapsed. The train was drawn by a 4-4-0 type locomotive designed by Thomas Wheatley in 1871. It was recovered from the river, repaired and remained in service with the North British Railway until 1919. The engraving on page 83 was from the cover of *The Penny Illustrated*. It was by Thomas Robinson, the father of that mechanical genius W. Heath Robinson.

1879 The Tay Bridge disaster 28 December 1879. The engraving
by Thomas Robinson is from *The Penny Illustrated.*
220×180 mm (approx).

DOWGATE WHARF,

LONDON.

Anthony Nichol & Son,

WHARFINGERS AND AGENTS.

Ships for

NEWCASTLE.   SUNDERLAND.

SHIELDS.   ALEMOUTH.

A Vessel clears every Wednesday & Saturday for Newcastle.

1820–60 Stock blocks, label and trade card. same size.

There are many sources of printed ephemera that have to do with shipping. The nineteenth century is particularly rich in posters, bills, manifests, invoices and letterheads that illustrate in one way or another the movement of shipping, the carriage of people and goods and the disasters that befell those who trusted their money, their wares or themselves to sailing vessels.

Thomas Bewick, the great Northumbrian wood engraver, as a young man made a passage to London in a Newcastle collier. The engraving on the left comes from his workshop, and may have been by his own hand.

Until the middle of the nineteenth century, the coastal trade was Britain's main source of transport for both people and goods. Small brigs and schooners were the usual carriers. On the east coast of England the Northumberland collier brigs sailed down to London on every tide. There were literally hundreds of these vessels afloat at the same time. For trans-Atlantic travel, the three-masted clipper ships, many times larger than the little coasters, were making the passage from Liverpool to Boston and still competing with the steamers.

Second-hand ships and boats were almost as common in the nineteenth century as are used cars today. Sometimes they were well found, 'handy little vessels . . . well adapted for the Coasting Trade' like the one Mr W. N. Heward of Sunderland offered for sale; more often they were broken-down, hog-backed old craft, or ones such as the *Defiance*, recently wrecked. The *Defiance* came to grief in 1839 on the beach just south of Hartlepool. This bill is clearly a proof, for the printer has corrected the spelling of 'canvas' and has pencilled in 'Of Stonehaven' below the word *Defiance*.

Custom's Clearances, charter parties and ship's manifests all give a picture of a ship's movements and of what she was carrying. The 79-ton schooner *Sylph* was built in Sunderland in 1842. By the date of these two forms on page 87, she was owned by Amos Howe of Woodbridge, the father of her skipper, John Howe.

The *Douanes Passe-Port* is interesting for various reasons; one is the typography with fine neo-classical borders, another that 'Empire Français', has been altered by hand to 'République Française'. The Second Empire had come to an end with the revolution of 1870, when the Third Republic was established and, with a war on its hands, had little time or even inclination to have new forms printed.

The *Sylph*, under her captain John Howe cleared for London. Two years later, whilst lying at Harwich, John Howe signed a charter party to carry a full cargo of wheat in bulk to Calais, Boulogne, Antwerp and Brussels.

1839 Wreck sale notice, printed by J. Procter, Hartlepool.
285 × 225 mm.

WRECKED VESSEL, &c.

HARTLEPOOL.

TO BE SOLD BY

Auction,

(For the benefit of the Underwriters)

On Friday the 8th of February, 1839,

On the Beach, about half Mile South of Hartlepool,

THE HULL OF THE WRECKED SCHOONER,

Defiance

(Burthen 60 Tons per Register admeasurement)

And all the MATERIALS and STORES saved from the said Wreck ;

Consisting of 2 lower Masts, Bowsprit, Jib Boom, Main ditto and Gaff, 3 Yards, Windlass, Rudder, Lower and Topmast Rigging, 2 Anchors, 1 Kedge, 1 Chain Cable, 1 Hemp ditto, 2 Warps, 1 Hawser, Topsail Sheet Chains, 1 Mainsail, 1 Topsail, 1 Royal sail, 20 coils of small Rope, several lots of Canvass, 1 Winch, 3 Metal Pumps, 1 new Stove, Cook's Copper, sundry Blocks, 2 Water Casks, Ballast Shovels, a quanlity of Deck Deals, &c.

Messrs. Sotheran, Auctioneers

N. B.   Sale to commmence at One o'clock.

PRINTED BY J. PROCTER, HARTLEPOOL.

FOR SALE

BY PRIVATE CONTRACT,

A HANDY LITTLE

VESSEL,

SLOOP RIGGED,

40 Tons Burthen; is well adapted for the Coasting Trade; the Hull has just undergone a thorough Repair, and is in good order. Two-thirds of the price would be taken in Barter.

For particulars apply to

W. N. HEWARD,

SHIP BROKER, SANS STREET.

Sunderland, 5th March, 1855.

W. B. Barnes, High Street, Bishopwearmouth.

1871 French clearance papers. The newly proclaimed republic is still using the Emperor Napoleon's official forms, though the royal coat of arms is defaced and the word 'Empire' replaced with 'République'.
210×150 mm (approx).

1873 Charter Party.
210×155 mm (approx).

Loss at sea was a recurring hazard and was recorded by posters, bills and the broadsheets of the ballad singers. The sinking of the paddle steamer *Rothsa Castle,* happened on 31 August 1831, when she struck a rock whilst on a day trip from Liverpool to Beaumaris. About a hundred souls perished. Mr Stephenson, printer of Gateshead, gives a moving description of this melancholy affair. His anonymous verse is worthy of McGonagall:

'All day they had been dancing, ne'er thinking of a gale,
But just to have a merry day and a pleasant sail.
When horrifying to relate the boat it struck a rock,
And roused them from their merriment by a most
dredful shock,
The children crying bitterly, hung round about their
necks,
And the wildest of despair might be seen upon the deck,
The rudder it was broken, the rest you well may guess,
For upwards of 100 were crying in distress,
Both from above and from below the boat was filling
fast,
Expecting every minute that it would be their last,
No aid there did come to them their precious lives to
save,
Oh, day of horror! oh, hapless day – they met a
watery grave.'

Stephenson, Printer, Gateshead

1838 Ballad sheet (top part only).
155×170 mm.

1840 *Rules and Orders for the Shipwrecked Seamen's Benevolent Society*, Woodbridge. Printed by J. Munro.
115×75 mm.

1878 Booklet published for Fortey's Wholesale Juvenile Book Warehouse, London.
160×103 mm.

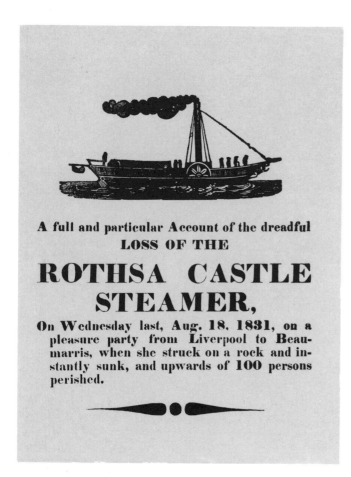

A full and particular Account of the dreadful
LOSS OF THE
ROTHSA CASTLE STEAMER,
On Wednesday last, Aug. 18, 1831, on a pleasure party from Liverpool to Beaumarris, when she struck on a rock and instantly sunk, and upwards of 100 persons perished.

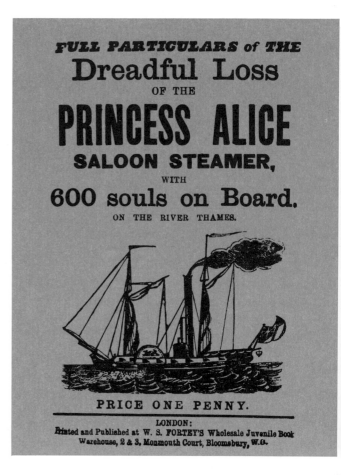

FULL PARTICULARS of THE
Dreadful Loss
OF THE
PRINCESS ALICE
SALOON STEAMER,
WITH
600 souls on Board.
ON THE RIVER THAMES.

PRICE ONE PENNY.

LONDON:
Printed and Published at W. S. FORTEY'S Wholesale Juvenile Book
Warehouse, 2 & 3, Monmouth Court, Bloomsbury, W.C.

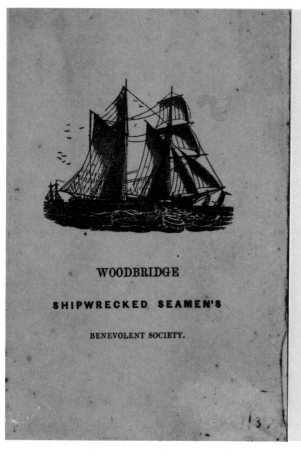

WOODBRIDGE

SHIPWRECKED SEAMEN'S

BENEVOLENT SOCIETY.

RULES AND ORDERS

FOR THE

GOVERNMENT

OF THE

SHIPWRECKED SEAMEN'S

BENEVOLENT SOCIETY,

HELD AT THE

ANCHOR INN, WOODBRIDGE,

In the County of Suffolk.

ESTABLISHED 1840.

WOODBRIDGE
PRINTED BY J. MUNRO, BOOKSELLER.

1840.

1912 Newspaper cutting: Wreck of the *Titanic*. Drawing by
Charles Dixon RI. From *The Daily Graphic* 20 April.
152×252 mm.

1912 Postcard issued to raise funds for the penniless orphans of
the *Titanic* disaster.
135×85 mm.

The 'Great Ship Company' share certificate at the top of page 90 is of interest, as it refers to the *Great Eastern*, which was designed by I. K. Brunel, the man who had surveyed the track for the Birmingham and Gloucester Railway (page 78). This great ship went through various financial difficulties from the time her keel was laid in December 1853 until her maiden voyage for the Eastern Steam Navigation Company on 7 September 1859, six months after the issue of this certificate, Brunel, the greatest engineer of his age, over-worked and worn out, had a stroke two days before his great ship set off for the east. He died a week later. The *Great Eastern*, successor to Brunel's equally revolutionary *Great Britain* was years ahead of her time, but she showed the way passenger ships were to develop. Until 1899 she was the largest ship in the world. She was the forerunner of the *Olympic* and the *Titanic*, the *Normandie* and Cunard's two great *Queens*.

On 20 April 1912 *The Daily Graphic* issued a supplement describing the horrors of the *Titanic* disaster.

The great White Star liner, the largest ship afloat, went to the bottom of the Atlantic, having struck an iceberg at 2.20 a.m. of 15 April.

The murky halftone reproduction of Charles Dixon's drawing, entitled 'How the *Titanic* was ripped from stem to stern by an iceberg' does not compare with the vitality of the wood engravings used in ephemeral printing a decade or so earlier.

The trade card for a passenger agency, the tickets for steamers, ferries and canal boats and the sailing notice for the 'Day boat between New York and Albany' were all printed in the USA between 1850 and 1870. The passengers travelling on this 'Day boat' paddle steamer *Armenia*, were entertained 'to the sweet cadences of the Calliope (a steam organ)' as they 'glide amid the most exquisite haunts of Nature'. The 150 mile journey took nine and a half hours upstream and half an hour less downstream.

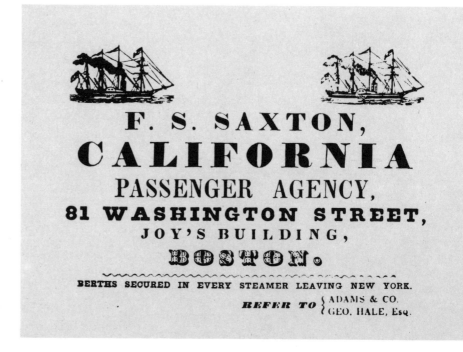

90

1850 Pass ticket for the New Jersey Ferry.
48 × 80 mm.

1853 Ticket for steamboat train and steamer.
43 × 70 mm.

c. 1860 Ticket for canal boat issued by the Western Line. *New York Public Library.*
43 × 64 mm.

c. 1870 Sailing notice. *New York Public Library.*
178 × 110 mm.

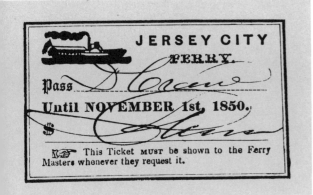

JERSEY CITY FERRY.

Pass

Until NOVEMBER 1st, 1850.

$

☞ This Ticket MUST be shown to the Ferry Masters whenever they request it.

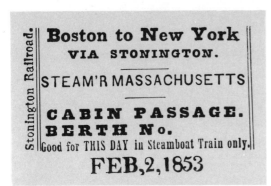

Stonington Railroad.

Boston to New York
VIA STONINGTON.

STEAM'R MASSACHUSETTS

CABIN PASSAGE.
BERTH No.

Good for THIS DAY in Steamboat Train only.

FEB, 2, 1853

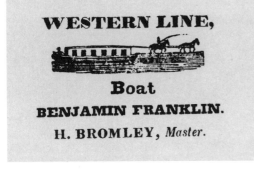

WESTERN LINE,

Boat
BENJAMIN FRANKLIN.

H. BROMLEY, *Master.*

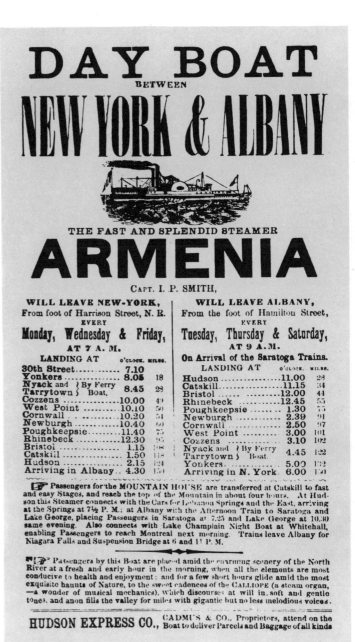

DAY BOAT
BETWEEN
NEW YORK & ALBANY

THE FAST AND SPLENDID STEAMER
ARMENIA
CAPT. I. P. SMITH,

WILL LEAVE NEW-YORK, From foot of Harrison Street, N. R. EVERY Monday, Wednesday & Friday, AT 7 A. M.		WILL LEAVE ALBANY, From the foot of Hamilton Street, EVERY Tuesday, Thursday & Saturday, AT 9 A. M. On Arrival of the Saratoga Trains.	
LANDING AT	O'CLOCK. MILES.	LANDING AT	O'CLOCK. MILES.
30th Street	7.10	Hudson	11.00 28
Yonkers	8.05 18	Catskill	11.15 34
Nyack and ⎱ By Ferry Tarrytown ⎰ Boat,	8.45 23	Bristol	12.00 44
Cozzens	10.00 40	Rhinebeck	12.45 55
West Point	10.10 50	Poughkeepsie	1.30 75
Cornwall	10.20 54	Newburgh	2.39 91
Newburgh	10.40 60	Cornwall	2.50 97
Poughkeepsie	11.40 75	West Point	3.00 101
Rhinebeck	12.30 95	Cozzens	3.10 102
Bristol	1.15 106	Nyack and ⎱ By Ferry Tarrytown ⎰ Boat,	4.45 122
Catskill	1.50 116	Yonkers	5.00 132
Hudson	2.15 124	Arriving in N. York	6.00 150
Arriving in Albany	4.30 150		

☞ Passengers for the MOUNTAIN HOUSE are transferred at Catskill to fast and easy Stages, and reach the top of the Mountain in about four hours. At Hudson this Steamer connects with the Cars for Lebanon Springs and the East, arriving at the Springs at 7½ P. M.; at Albany with the Afternoon Train to Saratoga and Lake George, placing Passengers in Saratoga at 7.25 and Lake George at 10.30 same evening. Also connects with Lake Champlain Night Boat at Whitehall, enabling Passengers to reach Montreal next morning. Trains leave Albany for Niagara Falls and Suspension Bridge at 6 and 11 P. M.

☞ Passengers by this Boat are placed amid the charming scenery of the North River at a fresh and early hour in the morning, when all the elements are most conducive to health and enjoyment; and for a few short hours glide amid the most exquisite haunts of Nature, to the sweet cadences of the CALLIOPE (a steam organ, —a wonder of musical mechanics), which discourses at will in soft and gentle tones, and anon fills the valley for miles with gigantic but no less melodious voices.

HUDSON EXPRESS CO., CADMUS & CO., Proprietors, attend on the Boat to deliver Parcels and Baggage of all kinds

The final stages of seaborne Atlantic travel were enacted by the great Cunard ships, the *Queen Mary* and the *Queen Elizabeth.* After that it was air transport and the Jumbo jets.

The two *Queens* were both over 80,000 tons and with the *Normandie* were the biggest passenger ships ever built. During the 1939–45 war, they ferried division after division of American troops across the Atlantic. By sleeping in three shifts, it was possible for over 15,000 service men to be carried on each voyage.

In comparison with the *Queens,* the little Furness Warren passenger-cargo liners *Newfoundland* and *Nova Scotia* looked like tug boats. They were of 7,436 tons and carried (at least the *Newfoundland* did on a voyage we made in her in 1958) thirty-five first-class passengers and sixty tourist class passengers. The *Newfoundland* and the *Nova Scotia* ran a shuttle service from Liverpool to St John, Newfoundland and Halifax, Nova Scotia and Boston and took thirteen days for the voyage. The ships were built in 1947 and provided, in their modest comfort, one of the most pleasant ways of crossing the Atlantic. They were fine sea boats.

1958 Passenger list of R.M.S. *Newfoundland*.
185×108 mm.

1958 Postcard of R.M.S. *Newfoundland*.
95×153 mm.

List of Passengers

FIRST CLASS

To ST JOHN'S, N.F.

Dr. P. I. Atkinson	Mrs. M. D. Gillespie
Mrs. Atkinson	Miss M. Redshaw
Miss J. P. Atkinson (9)	Miss T. E. Simpson
Master I. A. Atkinson (4)	Mrs. A. D. Townsend
Miss S. M. Burke	Master B. J. Townsend (11)
Miss C. Dunne	Major D. Wise

To HALIFAX, N.S.

Mr. W. A. Burtwell	Miss L. G. Cunningham (2)
Mrs. Birtwell	Miss C. Fleming
Mr. T. Coulter	Capt. A. H. Murray
Mrs. E. A. Cunningham	Mrs. M. S. Waugh

To BOSTON, MASS.

Mr. M. A. Barratt	Mrs. Ray
Mr. M. S. Bean	Mrs. B. L. Scherer
Mr. J. Burnett	Miss S. M. Snell
Mr. J. N. C. Lewis	Mr. J. B. Tate
Mrs. Lewis	Mr. L. G. D. Udall
Mr. C. F. Page	Mr. F. Wildin
Mrs. W. F. Quinlan	Mrs. N. J. Young
Dr. P. M. Ray	

1961 Folder containing accommodation plan for R.M.S. *Queen Elizabeth*.
215×95 mm.

1958 Folder containing accommodation plan for R.M.S. *Newfoundland*.
215×93 mm.

1961 Publicity leaflet for R.M.S. *Queen Elizabeth*.
41×195 mm.

Air travel

Printed ephemera is scattered about in the most prodigal way by modern air lines, though charter flight operators are rather less wasteful in this matter. The examples of ephemeral printing that pass through one's hands seem to be never-ending. At the airport, quite apart from the products and the packaging of duty-free goods, with their carrier bags, bills, stamps etc, there may be checks for meals and drinks. You could also buy postcards from the bookstalls, packaged sweets from the candy store, local papers from the newsvendors and so on.

On these next four pages I have skimmed the surface of two trips, one to Italy in 1972 and one to the USA and Canada in 1973. The Italian flights are recalled here by the printed ephemera over the page. The ticket indicates the outward flight was from Heathrow to Venice and the return flight was from Milan to Heathrow. There is a bus ticket for the bus journey from the West London Air Terminal to the airport, a boarding pass and the ubiquitous packet of sugar, with BEA's insignia. The most interesting item is the elaborate, multi-lingual flight bulletin, which was issued during the flight of Trident G.Arpe, as it was approaching Paris, flying at 600 m.p.h. at 29,000 feet. The Air Canada ticket was for a round trip from Heathrow to Kennedy Airport, from Bridgeport to Boston and from Boston to Toronto and Toronto back to Heathrow. The 'Welcome aboard' and 'Meet the Flying Staff' were from publicity literature in the seat pocket on the VC10. After spending a few days in Connecticut I flew from Bridgeport, the local airport, to Boston by Pilgrim Airlines in a high-winged monoplane. At Boston Logan International Airport, I took a return flight in a Down East Airlines Piper Commanche, which was about the size of a small shooting brake, to Rockland in Maine. I had two hours to wait before I could board the Down East Airlines plane, so I had lunch at the Space Room of the Logan International Airport, which rendered up a paper napkin, shown here, bill checks for cloakroom and drinks and the bill for the meal. I might have cadged a menu and a wine list and possibly the label off the bottle of wine, but I did not!

From Boston, I flew in an Allegheny Airliner to Toronto and amongst various excitements, which included the arrest at Buffalo of the passenger who was sitting next to me, the aircraft was struck by lightning as we were flying over Niagara Falls. Ten days later, I boarded for London a half-empty BOAC Boeing 747 Jumbo Jet, which is illustrated at the top of the colour page. The giant Boeing 747 flying at 30,000 feet made a nice contrast to the little Piper Commanche, which flew up the Maine coast at a bare 1,000 feet.

Commercial flying is still quite a romantic thing, and the collecting of these pieces of paper and the mounting of them up in sequence is one way of establishing, and later on recalling, the flavour of such flights. In the years ahead, such prodigal use of paper may, in a newly environmentally conscious world, become a thing of the past. But so may flying!

1973 Air travel ephemera.
331×257 mm.

Welcome aboard
British airways

BRITISH AIRWAYS – THE NEW IMAGE

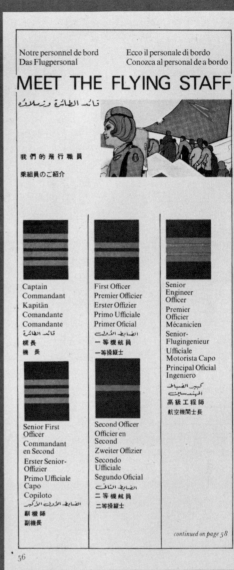

Notre personnel de bord
Das Flugpersonal

Ecco il personale di bordo
Conozca al personal de a bordo

MEET THE FLYING STAFF

قائد الطائرة وزملاؤه

我們的飛行職員

乗組員のご紹介

Captain
Commandant
Kapitän
Comandante
Comandante
قائد الطائرة
機長
機長

First Officer
Premier Officier
Erster Offizier
Primo Ufficiale
Primer Oficial
الضابط الأول
一等機航員
一等操縦士

Senior
Engineer
Officer
Premier
Officier
Mécanicien
Senior-
Flugingenieur
Ufficiale
Motorista Capo
Principal Oficial
Ingeniero
كبير الضباط المهندسين
高級工程師
航空機関士長

Senior First
Officer
Commandant
en Second
Erster Senior-
Offizier
Primo Ufficiale
Capo
Copiloto
الضابط الأول الأكبر
副機師
副機長

Second Officer
Officier en
Second
Zweiter Offizier
Secondo
Ufficiale
Segundo Oficial
الضابط الثاني
二等機航員
二等操縦士

continued on page 58

56

NEW YORK

BOAC
IDENTIFICATION TAG

387386

R CANADA

Passenger Ticket
and Baggage Check issued by:
Billet de Passage
et Bulletin de Bagages Emis par:
Air Canada

P
T

FLIGHT BA59

SEAT 26A

AIRCRAFT DOOR

BOAC BOARDING PASS

BEA | Flight Bulletin

Please pass on quickly
Prière de faire circuler rapidement
Si prega di far circolare sollecitamente
Bitte schnell weiterleiten
Por favor circule rápidamente

From Captain: *R Fisher*
Aircraft: *Trident G ARPH*

BRITISH EUROPEAN AIRWAYS

To all passengers	A tous les passagers	A tutti i passeggeri	An alle Fluggäste	A todos los pasajeros

You will find in front of you a booklet entitled 'about your flight'. You are requested to read the section on the use of the aircraft's safety equipment. Seat belts must be fastened before take-off.

Vous trouverez en face de vous une brochure intitulée 'votre vol'. Nous vous prions de lire le passage réservé à l'utilisation de l'équipement de sécurité installé à bord de l'avion. Vous êtes priés d'attacher vos ceintures avant le décollage.

Troverete di fronte a Vei un opuscolo intitolato 'about your flight'. Siete pregati di leggere la parte che si riferisce all'uso dell'equipaggiamento di emergenza dell'aereo. Le cinture di sicurezza devono essere allacciate prima del decollo.

In der Tasche an Ihrem Vordersitz finden Sie eine Broschüre mit dem Titel 'Ihr Flug'. Bitte lesen Sie den Absatz über den Gebrauch der an Bord befindlichen Sicherheitsausrüstung. Vor dem Start schnallen Sie sich bitte an.

Delante de Vd. encontrará un folleto titulado 'about your flight'. Por favor, lea el capítulo sobre el uso del equipo de seguridad del avión. Atese al cinturón del asiento antes del despegar.

When airborne you will be told when you may unfasten your seat belt and smoke (cigarettes only – no pipes or cigars, please). You will find the call button, the ventilators and the reading lights in the panel above the window.

En cours de vol, l'hôtesse vous annoncera quand vous pourrez détacher vos ceintures et fumer (des cigarettes seulement – veuillez, s'il vous plaît, ne fumer ni pipe ni cigare). Le bouton d'appel, les ventilateurs et les veilleuses se trouvent au-dessus du hublot.

Una volta in volo, sarete avvertiti quando potrete slacciare le cinture e fumare (solo sigarette; niente pipa o sigari per favore.) Troverete il pulsante di chiamata, il ventilatore e la luce da lettura al disopra del finestrino.

Sobald das Flugzeug die richtige Höhe erreicht hat, werden wir Ihnen sagen, dass Sie sich wieder abschnallen können. Auch das Rauchen ist dann wieder gestattet (aber bitte nur Zigaretten, keine Pfeifen oder Zigarren). Die Bedienungsklingel, Ventilatoren und Leselampe finden Sie über Ihrem Fenster.

Una vez en el aire se le indicará cuando podrá soltarse el cinturón del asiento y fumar (solo cigarillos – pipas o cigarros no, por favor). Hallará el timbre los ventiladores y las luces de lectura encima de la ventana.

English	Français	Italiano	Deutsch	Español			
Our height will be/is	Notre altitude sera/est de	La nostra altézza sarà/è de	Unsere Flughöhe	Debemos volar/volamos a una altura de	*27,000*		*8,500*
Our speed will be/is	Notre vitesse sera/est de	La nostra velocità sarà/è de	Unsere Fluggeschwindigkeit	Debemos volar/volamos a una velocidad de	*600*		*960*
We shall pass	Nous allons survoler	Passeremo	Wir werden überfliegen	Ahora vamos a pasar por	*Paris*		*1320*
Our next stop and approximate time of arrival (local time) are	Nous arriverons à la prochaine escale à l'heure approximative (heure locale)	Il prossimo scalo e Vi arriveremo alle circa (ora locale)	Unsere nächste Landung und ungefähre Landungszeit (Ortszeit) ist	Nuestra proxima escala y la hora aproximada de llegada (hora local) son	*Nice*		*1435*
Adjust your watch to local time at the next stop	Mettez votre montre à l'heure locale de la prochaine escale	Si regoli l'orologio secondo l'ora locale del prossimo scalo	Stellen Sie bitte Ihre Uhr bei der nächsten Landung nach der Ortszeit	Ajusten su reloj a la hora local en la proxima parada			
Your cabin attendants are	Vos commissaires de bord sont	I nomi del personale di cabina sono	Ihre Kabinenstewards sind	Sus auxiliares de vuelo son			
The traffic staff who will meet you on landing will be glad to assist you in any way they can	Le personnel d'escale qui vous accueillera à l'atterrissage sera heureux de vous aider dans toute la mesure du possible	Il personale di scalo che La ricevera all'arrivo sarà lieto di offrirle ogni assistenza	Das Boden— Abfertigungspersonal, das Sie bei der Landung erwartet, wird Ihnen gern in jeder Weise behilflich sein	El personal de trafico que estara en el aeródromo estara contento de poderles ayudar en todo cuanto sea posible			

T652 (2nd.)

1972 Air travel ephemera.
352 × 356 mm.

1973 Air travel ephemera.
363 × 272 mm.

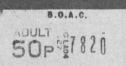

Name _____

Destination _____

Flight BA591

Form No. A3033 F

BOAC NEW YORK
JFK
FLIGHT
BA 591

BOSTON, MASS
PILGRIM AIRLINES
BAGGAGE CLAIM TAG
Pilgrim Airlines maximum limit of liability
is $250 per passenger or $250 per bag,
whichever limit is less.
0412-70381

BOS

01-76-78

FLIGHT
BOS
BOSTON, MASS.
01-76-78

pilgrim AIRLINES

BOS

ZAA
YYZ
FLIGHT
447
TORONTO 28-18-19

ALLEGHENY AIRLINES

PTD. U.S.A.

ALLEGHENY ®

ALLEGHENY AIRLINES
TORONTO
Baggage checked subject to tariffs, in-
cluding limitations of liability therein
contained.
This is not the check. baggage
check) described by article 4, of the
Warsaw Convention.

28-18-19

AIR CANADA ⊛ Montreal, Canada	ORIGIN/ORIGINE LONDON	DESTINATION LONDON	PASSENGER TICKET AND BAGGAGE CHECK Subject to Conditions of Contract (Page 2) NO. 2 BILLET DE PASSAGE ET BULLETIN DE BAGAGES Soumis aux Conditions de Transport (Page 3) FLIGHT COUPON COUPON DE VOL		014 404 913 531	

NAME OF PASSENGER / NOM DU PASSAGER
MR. J. LEWIS

FROM/TO DE/A	CARRIER TRANSPORT	FARE CALCULATION DÉCOMPTE			
LHR				DATE AND PLACE OF ISSUE	
JFK	BA	M		AIR CANADA MONTSAC	
BDR	PM	142.50		SEP 27 73	
BOS	PM				
YYZ	AL	145 BOP		LONDON 1	
LHR	MC	205.80			
YYZ				413.30	
LHR	G	15.00	DS 8	33.10	
		413.30			

GOOD FOR PASSAGE / VALABLE POUR LE TRANSPORT	FARE BASIS BASE TARIF.	CARRIER TRANSPORT	FLT./CLASS VOL./CLASSE	DATE	TIME HEURE	STATUS ÉTAT	FREE FRANCH	CARD PCS COLIS ENR	WT POIDS	UNCK.WT POS.NI STUF
LONDON	YUE21	BA	591	OCT12	1300	OK	2U	13	7	
NEW YORK	YUE21	AM	Q	P	E	N	2U			
BRIDGEPORT. CONN.	YUE21	PM	152A	OCT17	0545	OK	2U			
BOSTON	YUE21	AL	447S	OCT19	1150	OK	RUK			
TORONTO										

ORIGINAL ISSUE
014 9000 001 372 YYZ8 SEP 12 1473

TKT. TOUR CODE / CODE I.T.

FARE PRIX 144 40
TAX US 3.00
TAX US 3 140 40

ISSUED IN EXCHANGE FOR / EMIS EN ÉCHANGE DE
014 9000 001 372.

2 014 404913531 1

FORM OF PAYMENT / MODE DE PAIEMENT
NONREF !T! /AGT.

ISSUED IN CONJUNCTION WITH / BILLET COMPLEMENTAIRE
014 404 913 332.

FARE PRIX 444 40

TT74

DO NOT MARK OR WRITE IN WHITE AREA ABOVE / NE RIEN INSCRIRE DANS LA PARTIE BLANCHE CI-DESSUS

This flag WAS Hanging in marSA During the FIESTA →

BARCELONA Museo Pic...

Ermit... Sant Gregori-Falset

Diada Sant Gregori 1974

my Brorthers Toy paper →

ZAFARRANCHO DE COMBATE

LLorretDelmar WeSTopped HereAoon Our Way Home →

RENFE
NIÑO

These are my Holiday Tickets

ACEITE REFINADO DE SOJA

ACEITE GENEROSO

MAXIMIN GRUNHAUS

Maximin Grunhaus is a tiny village and a famous vineyard on the Ruwer which produces very fine wines in the good years especially. There are one hundred and twenty acres under vines most of them owned by a single family, the Von Schuberts. The vineyard is divided into several plots which are indicated on the label such as Maximin Grunhaus Herrenberg or Bruderberg ... ch.

The two labels (left and right) I have both come from the same vineyard plot the Herren... berg which means 'The lords or masters' hill' and both carry the same design. The difference is that one is off a bottle of wine and therefore has its neck label, the one is the label above right. It was off a bottle of wine from the 1964 vintage. The other label has not yet been stuck on a bottle and is from the famous year of 1959. The 1959 label I had some difficulty with in removing from the bottle and it is unfortunately slightly torn both on the main and the neck labels.

WALDRACH

Waldrach is a small town of secondary importance in the Ruwer. However it does produce some good quality wines from its more important vineyards the Mariaberg, Hubertusberg and Schloss Marienholz. The labels are from the Mariaberg and ... Hertusberg. They are both Riesling Spätleses and produced by Hagenbach. They show drawings of vineyards at Waldrach and have attractive grape and leaf designs on them in green and yellow.

EITELSBACH

Eitelsbach is a world famous little village on the Ruwer which produces wines of exceptional quality especially from the Karthäuser Hofberg vineyards (see over). The steep, splendid vineyards were m... ... was made in the great estate bottled and owned by the ...

... owned by a Carthusian Monastery but have now been, for over a century, the prope... Rautenstrauch family, and are still called Eitelsbacher Karthäuser Hofberg in "Carthusians hill". The other fairly noted vineyard in Eitelsbach is the Marien... I have on the opposite page below right. It is a good wine, a feine Auslese, and cask made, indicated by the cask number, Fuder Nr. 9203. The vine... by the Theological College in Trier and the money from the wine goes toward... Priests.

EITELSBACHER KARTHÄUS... HOFBERG

Owned by the famous family the Rautenstrauch... the Eitelsbacher Karthäuser Hofberg is one of the most famous vineyards in Germany. It covers an area of about seventy acres and is divided up into plots such as the Kronenberg, Burgberg, Sang and several othe... is a very small one and there is a joke that the ... with the longest name has the smallest ... appears to be true when you see all the ... manages to fit onto the labels with still ... left. The label above is one that ... taken off a bottle and comes from the Kronenberg plot from the 1953 vintage. The label above left is also from the Kronenberg but comes from the more recent 1967 vintage. The last label (below right) comes from the Burgberg plot and the great 1959 vintage. It is a feinste Auslese and was made by cask, (see cask no. Fd. Nr. 63). The paper from which the above label is ma... higher quality than the remaining two. This is probably because 1959 was such ... All three labels share the beautiful Rautenstrau... dominating the centre of the label.

AVESBACH

Avesbach is a small but im... on the Ruwer south of Trier ... high quality wines in the good y... (left) comes from the Hammerstein ... with the Herrenberg, Atterberg and Kupp ... more important vineyards. It is a Trockenbeeren... year 1959. It is also made by cask (see cask numb... ... state Domain. the label is of a very interesting th...

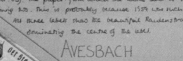

5. Printed Ephemera in Education

1974 Holiday task: scrap book describing a visit to Spain.
Courtesy Jackie Craig.
370×585 mm.

1971 Holiday task: German Wine Labels.
592×854 mm.

Printed ephemera has many uses as background material for essays, exercises and theses at different levels of education. A primary school exercise could be based on all the scraps of paper that the children could find on a day's outing to the seaside. These scraps could then be assembled in various ways, maybe to illustrate an hour-by-hour diary of the day's events.

Mrs Jackie Craig, a young and imaginative teacher, inspired eight-year old Christian Barker, a pupil at Highbury Quadrant Junior School in London, to record his summer holiday near Tarragona in Spain in a scrap book, by collecting every scrap of paper that came his way. He succeeded in assembling a colourful mixture of sweet papers, bullfight posters, matchbox covers, printed festival ribbons, paper flags, menus, tickets and posters. The colourful illustration opposite this page is taken from pages in Christian's scrapbook. It is both evocative and artlessly decorative.

Another subject that might appeal to children could be the life of their favourite pop star, which could be made up from record sleeves, gramophone company handouts and pictures torn from the pages of *The Melody Maker* and other journals. For students at university and college, printed ephemera's back-up possibilities are legion. Graphic design students have a natural aptitude for using such material. Recent theses that I have seen have included one using ephemera to illustrate a history of canals, an essay on litho-stone images and a study of the German wine trade. This last one was in fact done by Charlotte Don, a fourteen-year old Benenden schoolgirl.

Charlotte produced for her school 'hobby task', a survey of German wine labels. Admittedly she was working in the right ambience, for her father is a Master of Wine. With some slight help from this quarter Charlotte set to work on her album. She says she became interested in wine labels when she was only ten years old. She used to soak labels off wine bottles and stick them on the walls of her playroom. She turned this decorative use to something more profound when she decided to make up an album of labels and write something about them. The amount of material available was intimidating, but after some reflection, she decided that the German labels were the most beautiful and as she was also doing German at school, it seemed the most logical area in which to work.

Her father's help was actually limited to telling her which were the most important estates in each of the German wine districts and giving her addresses to which to write. He also gave her the run of his library. Here she found three different books that gave her much of the background.

Charlotte wrote off to the various estates and shippers, asking for information and specimens of their labels. Her thesis begins with a lucid explanation of German wine names and with remarkable judgement, the first label she shows is one designed for the shippers Langenbach & Co by O.M. Hadank the greatest of all modern wine label designers.

The two pages shown here make up the last spread in Charlotte Don's album. She shows two versions of the floridly beautiful labels for Maximin Grünhauser Herrenberg, pointing out that the one with a neck label is off a bottle of the 1966 vintage and that the other has yet to be stuck on to a bottle of the famous 1959 vintage. On the opposite page she shows three examples of the exquisite Eitelsbacher Karthäuser Hofberg. Charlotte concludes her account by remarking that this is the smallest label used for a German wine with the longest name!

The history of canals was beautifully produced by Sally-Ann Webb, a student at the Newport College of Art. In describing the decline of the canals she showed, among other pieces of ephemera, an 1853 notice announcing the closure of the Carlisle Canal Navigation. She also has an 1886 notice issued by the Leeds office of the Aire and Calder Navigation about the finding of 'Drowned persons'. A reward of five shillings was given for reporting such a find, and a fine of £5 for not reporting it! Miss Webb also used modern notices and advertisements to illustrate present-day uses, such as 'A Holiday to remember . . .' for pleasure cruising on the river Shannon and another for the Trent Valley Cruising Hotel with 'specially designed *wide* beam Hotel Boat, operating on routes of historic interest on the wider canals and rivers'. Such pieces of ephemera are valuable illustrative material both for their typographic idiosyncrasies and for their actual content.

Bob Bain, a diploma student at Gray's School of Art, Aberdeen, produced an interesting thesis on 'the Lithographic Stone Image'. This was based on the relics of a firm of Aberdeen printers whose old factory had closed down after they had been amalgamated with two other firms. The relics took the form of about 800 lithographic stones and a collection of labels which had been in storage for over seventy years. One of the post-diploma students at Grays' realized their historic interest and with the help of a group of students removed a number of these stones to a newly founded print workshop called Peacock Printers.

The stones were cleaned by the students, re-etched and then proofed. The subjects revealed were wax candles, ginger beer, smoked sprats, birdseed and a great variety of billheads. The labels were for Demarara Rum and Stewart's Trade Wind Rum, Clan Blend Whisky, Findon Haddock, Peerless Lemon Peel, Marshall's Brisling, Marshall's Cod Roes and Marshall's Kippered Herrings and Baxter's Royal Game Soup. Bob Bain's thesis was a thirst-inspiring affair. It was also, thanks to this material, a graphic reflection of local industries, the chief of these being fishing and whisky distilling.

One could cite many other uses of printed ephemera in an educational context but these examples should be enough to point the direction to *Jackdaws* and to the *History at Source* books.

In 1962, Tony Colwell, of the London publishing firm of Jonathan Cape, produced for advertisement purposes and bookshop display a foolscap wallet containing facsimiles of documents, cartoons and printed matter to do with John Stanhope's book *The Cato Street Conspiracy*. 'John Stanhope' was the pseudonym of John Langdon-Davis.

Langdon-Davis, a visually-minded author who, under Stefan Lorant had served his time as a journalist on *Picture Post*, had a strong belief in the use of visual material for teaching. He showed this *Cato Street* folio to his schoolmaster friend Raymond Groom. Groom's response was that however useful it might be for bookshop advertising, it would be even more useful as a teaching aid.

John Langdon-Davis went home to consider the matter. Eventually he prepared several dossiers containing printed ephemera and other material, with the idea of going to an educational publisher. Whilst working on these, he appealed to Michael Howard at Cape for advice about methods of production. Cape were not educational publishers, but Michael Howard and his colleagues became intrigued with the idea of these wallets of information and decided to publish them themselves.

A trial dossier was actually produced at Cape by Andrew Thomson, their one-man printing department, working on a small offset machine in the basement of Cape's office in Bedford Square. They costed the operation and found that they could sell the dossier for 45p. They named the dossiers *Jackdaws*, after the collecting habits of those acquisitive birds.

The first one to be published was *The Battle of Trafalgar* and two others were published immediately afterwards. This was in December 1963. Forty other 'forthcoming titles in preparation' were listed on the back of this first trio. 'This was a bluff to discourage immediate imitation,' Michael Howard wrote later on. The bluff worked, though one firm of paper merchants produced one or two impressive pieces of advertising in the same form as *Jackdaws*. By 1974, 130 *Jackdaws* had been published, covering history, geography and science. There was also a French, an American and a Canadian series. The subjects were very varied and included *Magna Carta, The Slave Trade, Voyages of Captain Cook, Winston Churchill, The Early Trade Unions, The Great Exhibition 1851, The Easter Rising: Dublin 1916, Christmas, Pasteur and the Germ Theory, Ned Kelly, Lenin, The Brontës, Weekend à Paris, Building of the Canadian Pacific Railway* and *The California Gold Rush*.

It is an impressive selection and ephemeral printing played a big part in the contents of all these wallets. Clearly it should be possible for children to build up their own dossiers, but of course the choice of subject would depend on whether original material and copying facilities were available. The possibilities are almost endless and probably the greatest educational value comes from the research involved.

One of the greatest contributions that printed ephemera has made to education is in the *History at Source* books that another London publisher, Evans Brothers, have produced. Three of these books are by Robert Wood and they are titled *Children 1773–1840, Law and Order 1725–1886* and *Entertainments 1800–1900*. Many of the illustrations are from Mr Wood's own collection of ephemeral printing. This collection came from the spike files of a printer in West Hartlepool. Mr Wood first showed a selection of this ephemera in his *Victorian Delights*, which was published by Evans Brothers in 1967.

Robert Wood remarked in a letter to the author that printed ephemera are easier to work on (for students) than manuscript material, for the very good reason that 'a man has to concentrate his thoughts and arrange his material if he ventures into print'. He continued: 'In Victorian times printing was cheap and most announcements, controversies and propaganda were carried on through posters and pamphlets. Ballads about local disasters at sea or in the collieries were still being printed, every little society or benefit club had its notices and rules printed. Auctioneers bills provide almost as much information about contemporary furnishing (in their lists of the contents of houses) as did mediaeval wills.'

The *History at Source* books can be used in various ways. The books are so bound that they can be taken to pieces and the pages studied individually, just as if they were the original 'Wanted for Murder' or '50 Guineas Reward for the Apprehension of a Felon' bills. They can also be used as an inspiration for students to seek out comparable material for themselves.

The *Jackdaws* and the *History at Source* books point the way. There is an almost unlimited field for educational use in contemporary ephemera, whether it be turgid government notices about income tax or the rising cost of the postal services, or posters for horror movies or church bazaars or the printed wraps of blood-red 'Dracula ice lollies' or packs of '1p off' detergents. This material, however trivial is 'the very stuff of history today'.

Another comparable use was demonstrated by the popular author Dennis Wheatley in the 1930s. Wheatley wrote one or two thrillers which were presented in the form of police dossiers, with documents, bus tickets and other printed papers as potential clues. They brought new element into fiction.

1974 Lithographed letterheading and labels, c. 1900, taken from
lithographic stones that had been in store over seventy years.
Printed at Grays School of Art Aberdeen.

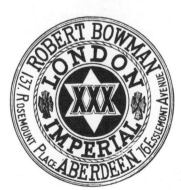

6. Woodbridge: A small town during the nineteenth century

In the nineteenth century Woodbridge, which lies at the head of an estuary some nine miles from the sea, was a seafaring town depending on shipping and ship building for its well being. The names of the pubs, the *Mariner's Arms,* the *Ocean Monarch*, the *Anchor* and the *Plough and Sail* reflected this salty background. Many of the tradesmen had shares in the Woodbridge ships and many more supplied their needs as ship builders and repairers, ropemakers, sailmakers and ship chandlers. The main trade was the export of wheat and the import of coal. The depression in agriculture, the coming of the railway in 1859 and finally road transport killed the trade of the little port.

Printed ephemera can show a vivid picture of the life of such a place. It can also show how a provincial town reacted to national events, even though the day-to-day happenings of the town and surrounding countryside played a much bigger part in the lives of the people. In the relatively placid days of England in the nineteenth century a royal wedding or a royal funeral was an excuse for festivities or a day off, when days off were a rarity and playing marbles on a Sunday could be treated as a felony and result in fearful penalties.

The first event to be celebrated here, somewhat prematurely in 1814, is peace, a year before Waterloo finally brought Bonaparte's ambitions to an end. It is a bookish little notice, in some contrast to the lively Vestry notice of four years later. With the introduction of bold display type faces in the early years of the nineteenth century, notices and posters changed in appearance from looking like pages out of books to something typographically original, rich and bold.

In 1820 a sombre little bill was issued as a result of a Vestry meeting announcing the closure of all shops and places of business on the day of the funeral of 'His late revered Majesty', King George III. Vestry meetings play a recurring part in the life of Woodbridge. The town celebrated the Coronation of the Prince Regent as George IV with a 'Festival'. Some short time afterwards a Loyal Address was printed, as a result of the accusations of infidelity that the King was now throwing at his unfortunate wife, whom he had long since forsaken. The King's proposal for a bill for the dissolution of his marriage had to be abandoned because of such public agitation, however mealy-mouthed this address may seem.

Concerts were held, 'Under the Patronage of the Nobility and Gentry', 'A New Song' was printed about a recurrence of the Luddite Riots, and Woodbridge had another Festival in 1832, this time to celebrate the passing of the Reform Bill. Of the various notices printed in Woodbridge in 1832, one is headed CAUTION and warns 'Reformers . . . who have been insulted as the supporters of Tom Paine, Cobbett, etc. not to solicit a Single Penny from their Purses (that is, of those who would belatedly join their ranks)'. It is signed by 'A Real Reformer'. Late in the year an Election is looming up and the Whigs and Tories have a printed slanging match.

1820 Public Notice. Funeral of George III. Printed by S. Loder, Woodbridge.
273 × 224 mm.

PARISH
OF
Woodbridge.

At a Vestry Meeting held this Day, pursuant to Public Notice,

IT was unanimously agreed by the Inhabitants present, to suspend all Business, and to keep the Shops closed on the Day appointed for the Funeral of his late revered Majesty King GEORGE the THIRD, which is expected to take place on Wednesday next, the 16th instant, and the MARKET will be held on

TUESDAY,
Previous to the usual Market-Day.

February 10th, 1820.

[S. LODER, PRINTER AND BOOKSELLER.]

1814 Notice of Public Dinner. Printed by S. Loder, Woodbridge.
247 × 187 mm.

1818 Notice of Election of Churchwardens. Printed by Smith and
Co. Woodbridge.
283 × 225 mm.

1819 Notice about Casual Relief. Printed by S. Loder, Woodbridge.
183 × 222 mm.

WOODBRIDGE,

11th JULY, 1814.

IT having been intimated by a number of respectable Persons of this Town, that a Public
Dinner should be given to celebrate the happy
return of PEACE, and to commemorate the
late numerous splendid Achievements of our
ARMY and NAVY, after a long and arduous
struggle, ending so honorable to our Country;
and that while every breast swells with national exultation from their eminent Services,
the principal Inhabitants might, as well as
their poorer Brethren, impress on their minds
Events so great and glorious.

Such Gentlemen, Tradesmen, and others who are
inclined to give their support to this Entertainment, are
invited and respectfully solicited to leave their Names at
Mr. SHEMING's, Mr. MILES', Mr. EDWARDS, or Mr.
CANA's, on or before *Wednesday* next, by Twelve o'clock,
in order that Stewards may be appointed, and arrangements made on a scale liberal and appropriate to the
occasion.

☞ It is submitted that Tickets should be 12s. each.

Printed by S. Loder, Bookseller.

PARISH
OF
WOODBRIDGE,

At a Vestry Meeting held this Easter Monday, the 23rd of March, 1818.

MR. THOMAS GRIMWOOD,
AND
MR. EDWARD LODER,

Were unanimously elected Churchwardens of this Parish for the Year ensuing.

The thanks of the Meeting were unanimously voted to the late Churchwardens,
MESSRS. LEEK, and GRIMWOOD, for
their great exertions for the benefit of the
Parish during the two last years.

☞ *Dinner at the Crown Inn this day at four o'Clock.*

SMITH AND CO. LETTER-PRESS AND COPPER-PLATE PRINTERS.

NOTICE.

WOODBRIDGE, *May 20th*, 1819.

*At a Meeting of the Parish-Officers last Evening, it was unani-
mously agreed,*

THAT a Weekly Publication of the Names, Situations and Earnings
of Applicants for casual Relief, with the Assistance afforded them,
should be placed on the Doors of the Church and other Public Places of
Worship, in order, that while the really necessitous Poor are relieved,
deceptions and impositions by false statements may be discovered, and
the Parish protected, as much as possible, from unnecessary burthens;---
We do therefore hereby give Notice, That the said Publication will commence the ensuing Week.

THOMAS TEMPLE SILVER, *Visitor.*
JONATHAN TURNER, } *Guardians.*
WILLIAM PATTISSON, }

[*S. Loder, Printer and Bookseller.*]

The Henneker and Broke Election Notices were in connection with the first election after the passing of the Reform Bill. The Tory cry was 'England flourished more during Tory Wars than she does now during a Whig Peace'. According to the Tories all that the Whigs had done was to empty the Treasury, feather their own nests, give £5,000,000 to the Emperor of Russia and put a German boy on the throne of Greece – and all this to be paid out of British taxes.

In 1840 some humourist published a verse, printed in heavy type within black borders, bemoaning the fact that Woodbridge had failed to rise to the occasion of Queen Victoria's marriage to Prince Albert of Saxe-Coburg-Gotha, even though five years earlier the town had celebrated the introduction of gas light to their theatre with a splendid variety performance (sponsored by the manager of the gas company!). In the same theatre a few years later they were still re-enacting the 1797 *Mutiny at the Nore.*

On 13 August 1846 Woodbridge was again turning its attention to its own private fun, with an annual regatta which included a duck hunt in addition to sailing and rowing matches, followed in the evening by a firework fête.

The middle of the century passed quietly enough but in 1873 a visit to Woodbridge on 20 December of the Prince and Princess of Wales called forth this comment from the local paper:

'Royal visits here now-a-days are like angels, few and far between. They used not to be so when George IV was Prince Regent and George III King. There were no railways in those days; the mediocracy and the democracy were accustomed to travel by stage coach and stage wagon and the aristocracy in their private coaches or post chaises, drawn by relays of post horses from stage to stage. Then it was that the Prince Regent, the Duke of Wellington and other illustrious personages used to visit Sudbourne Hall, the Marquis of Hertford's shooting lodge, changing horses at the Crown Hotel.

'When the Reform Bill swept away the right of the Boro' of Orford to return members to Parliament, the Marquis of Hertford deserted his shooting box at Sudbourne and royal visits were in consequence, discontinued, and until last Saturday no Royal countenance has honoured Woodbridge with its presence.'

All this because a royal couple were visiting Rendlesham Hall and had graciously agreed to catch the train from Woodbridge. The end of the Rotten Boroughs was not welcomed by the tradesmen of Woodbridge, it had meant a considerable loss of trade.

The royal train consisted of the royal saloon, a family saloon, two composite carriages, two brakes and a carriage trunk. The royal train was detached from the ordinary train and sent on as a special, arriving at Bishopsgate at 3.15, 'true to the minute': from Ipswich it took one and three quarter hours.

THEATRE, WOODBRIDGE.

On Thursday, March 7th,

Will be performed Jerrold's popular Comedy, called The

WEDDING GOWN

Mathew Lubeski, Mr. LEMMON—Beeswing, Mr. C. FISHER
Clarendon, Mr. FISHER—Effingham Mr. CHAPMAN
Creamly, Mr. G. FISHER—Trunket, Mr. FENTON
Valise, Mr. TWIDDY

Augusta, Miss COPPIN—Margaret, Mrs. FISHER
Lady Aubrey, Mrs. HODGSON—Mrs. Fossil, Miss C. ATKINSON

After which (for the only time) the celebrated Drama, of

THE MUTINY
AT
THE NORE
Or, British Sailors in 1797.

Captain Arlington (Captain of the Sandwich) Mr. CHAPMAN
Richard Parker (President of the Delegates at the Nore) Mr. LEMMON
Jack Adams (able Seaman aboard the Sandwich) Mr. FENTON
Timothy Bubble (late Clerk in Portsmouth Dock Yard, now Farmer in the Isle of Grain) Mr. G. FISHER
Dicky Chicken (Bubble's Factotum) Mr. C. FISHER
Captain Davis (of the Marines) Mr. TWIDDY
Mary Parker (Wife of Richard Parker) Miss COPPIN
Mrs. John Adams, Miss C. ATKINSON
Dame Grouse (Housekeeper to Bubble) Mrs. HODGSON
Sailors, Marines, &c.

In the course of the Piece, the following Scenery, &c.

QUARTER DECK OF THE SANDWICH.
VIEW OF THE ISLE OF GRAIN.
SECOND VIEW OF THE ISLE OF GRAIN.
Cabin in the Sandwich.
DECK OF THE SANDWICH.
With Preparations for Execution, &c.

On MONDAY, March 11th,
New and Popular Performances,
FOR THE BENEFIT OF
Mr GEORGE,
Box-book Keeper.

Boxes, 3s. 6d.—Upper Boxes, 2s. 6d.—Pit, 2s.—Gallery, 1s.
Children under Ten, Boxes, 2s. 6.—Upper Boxes, 2s.—Pit, 1s. 6d.
Second Price, Boxes, 2s.—Upper Boxes, 1s. 6d.—Pit, 1s.—Gallery, 6d.
Doors to be opened at Six, and the Performance to commence at ½ past.

God save the King!

WOODBRIDGE FESTIVAL.

IN HONOUR OF THE

CORONATION OF KING GEORGE THE FOURTH,

THURSDAY, JULY 19th, 1821,

A Public Dinner

Will be given to 500 Old People and Children, on the Lawn of GEORGE THOMAS, Esq. precisely
at One o'clock; and at Three o'clock the following

Rustic Sports and Amusements

WILL COMMENCE:

A JUMPING MATCH,

By Twelve Men, or not less than Eight,

Each man to jump in a good 4-bushel sack (to be provided by himself) the distance of 100 yards,
for a Hat, which will be given to the winner.

A Grinning Match,

THROUGH HORSE COLLARS, FOR A QUARTER-OF-AN-HOUR,

By Six Men, for a Pair of Shoes, (each Man to provide himself with a Collar) which will be
given to the winner, and 2s. 6d. to the second best.

A SPINNING MATCH,

By Three Old Women, for a Pound of Tea, (each Woman to provide herself with a Wheel) the
Wool will be furnished by the Stewards, and the prize adjudged by a competent person.

A BOBBING MATCH,

By Six Boys, for Five Shillings,

Six earthen pans will be provided by the Stewards, and Sixpence deposited in each with some
Flour, and the Boy who shall first take out the Sixpence with his mouth (having his hands tied
behind him) shall receive the above Prize, and the second boy doing the same shall receive 2s. 6d.

A Jingling Match,

BY NOT LESS THAN TEN MEN,

For a good Cheese, and 2s. 6d. the Man who catches the Jingler to receive the first Prize, but if
the Jingler is not caught in half-an-hour, he is to receive both prizes. Each man is to be blindfolded, and placed at equal distances from the Jingler before starting.

A CLIMBING MATCH,

For a Hat placed on the top of a Pole, the first person that reach the top to be entitled to the Hat.

A WHEELBARROW RACE,

BY SIX MEN BLINDFOLDED, FOR A PAIR OF SHOES.

The above Prizes will be determined by the Stewards, appointed for that purpose.
The Names of Persons for the above Sports, to be entered at Mr. GALL's, Druggist, on or before Wednesday Evening.
A. B. No Person will be allowed to go inside the Ropes during the time of Dinner, except such as are appointed to keep the
ground clear.

[J. LODER, Printer, Bookseller, and Stationer.]

Loyal Addresses.

LAYING FOR SIGNATURES AT MR. SMITH'S, PRINTER AND BOOKSELLER.

TO THE

KING'S MOST EXCELLENT MAJESTY.

SIRE,

WE, your Majesty's dutiful and Loyal Subjects, Inhabitants of the town of WOODBRIDGE, in the county of Suffolk, humbly beg leave to approach your Throne, with the expression of our firm attachment to your sacred person, to the laws and constitution of these realms, and to the principles which triumphed when the Crown was entrusted to your august family.

At this momentous crisis, when a formidable conspiracy to bring royalty into contempt, has been on the verge of success; when the daring hand of innovators has been outstretched to subvert the old safeguards of personal freedom, by the introduction of an *ex post facto* law and strange mode of trial; when the dearest charities of our nature have been insulted by the persecution of " the "wretched, and one who had none to help her"—and when our holy religion has been blasphemed by a contempt of its most venerable and endearing sanctions.—We feel it our duty to assure your Majesty that our hearts are untouched by the influences of that reckless profligacy which has violated the constitution and endangered the Throne.

We offer therefore to your Majesty, our humble and hearty congratulations on the defeat of these machinators, who in the degradation of your royal Consort would not only have perpetrated an unparalleled act of injustice, but moreover would have stricken at the inmost principle of that hereditary government, which we trust may long resist the outrages of faction and protect the virtue, the arts, and the energies of a free people.

Listen not Sire ! We humbly implore you, to those who would divert your indignation from the *real* enemies of your Crown, by traducing your faithful Subjects—to those who find crime in their expressions of agony—atheism in their freedom of thought—treason in the honest sympathies of their manly hearts.

Aroused indeed they are,—but it is not in military array, but in the quiet dignity of intellectual power.—Their loyalty is not a desire of place, but an attachment to your august family, as the chosen and legitimate guardians of equal laws.

Their religion is not a thing of state expediency, which looks for its reward in human palaces, but an unbending principle which directs its hopes to " temples not made " with hands, eternal in the heavens."—Their patriotism is not a selfish attachment to a selfish faction, but a child-love to their country's soil, a rational conviction of the excellence of its constitution, and a pride in those illustrious men whom its freedom has produced, and in those virtues which its continued freedom alone can secure.

We humbly pray you, Sire ! To dismiss from your councils those Ministers who have shewn themselves unequal to direct the energies of this great nation; who have pressed it almost to earth by taxation;—who have mocked its sympathies;—and replied to its petitions by the sabre ! Now, that after so many sad successes, they are defeated and disgraced; we implore your Majesty to confide in them no longer. Trust not, Sire ! to those who would slander and oppress your subjects, and heap the weight of their own iniquities on your Crown, but to those vast multitudes who while they petition for a change of councils, unite their prayer with ours, that your Majesty may long reign, the revered Sovereign of a free and virtuous people !

TO THE

QUEEN'S MOST EXCELLENT MAJESTY.

May it please Your Majesty,

WE, Inhabitants of the town of WOODBRIDGE, in the county of Suffolk, beg leave to approach your Majesty with our heartiest congratulations on the defeat of the last *atrocious conspiracy*, to despoil you of your rights and of your honour. When we consider the prospects with which your Majesty first came to our shores; the unhappy circumstance which so soon deprived you of the protection of your husband; the long and vexatious persecutions with which your retirement was invaded; and that mysterious visitation of Divine Providence by which you were made childless.—We cannot express the indignation which we feel at the attempt to aggravate your sufferings and deprive you of those dignities for which you paid no less a price, than the happiness of your life.

As Men, we despise the spirit which could thus treat a bereaved and disconsolate Woman.—As friends to loyalty, we mourn the folly which would have deprived it of one whose nobleness of nature and kindness of heart, fit her to adorn the Throne.—As Christians, we grieve for the reckless policy which set at nought the sacredness of the marriage tie, and the plainest dictates of the Word of God.

Nor were the means employed by your Majesty's enemies less unworthy than the end which they sought.

To effect your destruction the OLD LAWS of the realm were disregarded.—A new mode of trial sanctioned.—*Accusers* constituted jurors and judges,—and those advantages denied which parties accused of treason may claim, which are powerful to protect the innocent, but offer no shield to the guilty. Week after week, we beheld the most AUGUST ASSEMBLY in the World, insulted by a *tissue of perjuries* industriously collected from the *vilest corners of Italy !* In direct opposition to the eternal laws of nature : and calculated to shed polluting influences throughout the people; and to debase our Country in the eyes of the World.—We rejoice that all this varied machinery;—all the power of Ministers;—all the bad passions of discarded menials;—all the weight of power and all the subtleties of meanness, have wrought nothing but their own villany.—Your Majesty has not appealed to the heart of this great people in vain. The character of Englishmen, the rights of the subject; the honours of your sex, have all triumphed in your victory.

May your Majesty long live to enjoy the affections and to receive the blessings of the noble minded Nation, in whom you have so generously trusted ! And may the history of your triumph then convince Governors that the voice of the people uplifted in a righteous cause, has irresistible power to awe the oppressor into justice !

1826 Publication notice. Printed by J. Munro, Woodbridge.
240×192 mm.

TO ALL WHO HAVE THE INTEREST OF

IGNORANCE & BIGOTRY AT HEART,

This Statement is addressed.

AND IT IS HOPED THEIR TENDER AND COMPASSIONATE SYMPATHY MAY BE BESTOWED

ON THE

ILLUSTRIOUS OBSCURE,

WHO INTEND

SHORTLY TO EXPOSE THEMSELVES.

ALTHOUGH in this large and populous County there are no less than Four Weekly Journals extant, yet it is presumed sufficient room is now left for the establishment of a fifth, of Selfish and Servile Principles,—unconnected with any liberal Party,—the Proprietors of which are bound by no ties, except those of Ignorance and Bigotry, and a determined support, as far as in their power lies, of the Interests and Welfare of both.—" *Mus in Pice*," is the Motto of their Editor.

THE DARK LANTHORN,

Or, Suffolk Twinkler, and Woodbridge Farthing Rush=light,

Will be published Weekly, commencing about the middle of September next; and few subjects on which meddling folly can commit itself, will pass without their appropriate blunder. The chuckles and shrugg'd shoulders which this proposition has exacted in all quarters (*especially the most respectable,*) convince the Proprietors their prospect of affording mirth is well founded, and they pledge themselves that nothing shall remain undone on their part to justify the general presentiment. Further particulars will shortly appear.

HUMPHREY HIGGINBOTTOM & Co.

WOODBRIDGE. SUFFOLK,
July 13th, 1826.

J. MUNRO, PRINTER, AND BOOKSELLER, WOODBRIDGE.

Under the Patronage of the Nobility and Gentry.

GRAND CONCERT

OF

VOCAL AND INSTRUMENTAL MUSIC,

TO BE HELD AT THE ASSEMBLY ROOM,

CROWN TAVERN, WOODBRIDGE,

ON TUESDAY, OCTOBER 6th, 1829.

PRINCIPAL PERFORMERS.

A LADY OF IPSWICH,

MR. SPORLE,
From the Argyle Rooms, London.

MR. G. F. REYNOLDS,
From the Theatre Royal, Cheltenham,

AND MR. BRADDOCK.

PART I.

OVERTURE.—"Tancredi" .... *Rossini.*	SONG.—Mr. G. F. Reynolds, "Serenade Isabelle" *Bayley.*
SONG.—Mr. Sporle, "Highland Minstrel Boy" *Barnett.*	SONG.—Mr. Sporle, "Minstrel Knight".............. *Dussek.*
DUET.—A Lady and Mr. G. F. Reynolds, "I love thee" .... *Bishop.*	SONG.—A Lady, "Love from the Heart"
	GLEE.—A Lady, Mr. Sporle, & Mr. Braddock *More*

PART II.

OVERTURE. .... *Haydn.*	GLEE.—A Lady, Mr. Sporle, and Mr. G. F. Reynolds
SONG.—Mr. Sporle, "Rise Gentle Moon"........ *Barnett·*	POLLACCA.—Mr. G. F. Reynolds, "No more by Sorrow"................... *Braham.*
SONG.—Mr. G. F. Reynolds, "Maid of Llangollen" *Clark.*	SONG.—Mr. Sporle, "Meet me by Moonlight" *Wade.*
DUET.—Mr. Sporle and G. F. Reynolds, "When thy Bosom" .... *Brhaam*	FINALE.—Instrumental Overture Figaro .... *Mozart.*

To conclude with Mr. Reynolds's **DRAMATIC MELANGE,** *as delivered by him in his Tour through England, Ireland, and Wales.*

MODERN TRAVELLING.

Off by the Mail—Description of Passengers—Miss Moneyballs, daughter of a Pawnbroker, wanting to stop the Coach—Fur-cap Comfort—Nothing like it.

SONG,—"CRACK WHIP AND DASH AWAY."

JOURNEY CONTINUED.

Utility of a Snuff-box—Politeness not always agreeable—French Explanation—English Replies—Frenchman Puzzled—How to please a Husband—Four-and-Twenty the topic of Conversation.

SONG,—"FOUR-AND-TWENTY ROYAL VISITORS."

Mr. Pompous, Signs of Contentment—Mr. Dismal, Signs of Disappointment—Anxiety for one's Family—Comfortable Calculations—Dangers of a Safety Coach—Parish Meetings for the good of the Poor.

SONG,—"THE CHURCHWARDEN'S DINNER."

To conclude with a Digression on the Study of the Law—Goody Grym *versus* Lapstone—Yorkshireman in search of a Civilian—Family Anecdote, and Visit to Windsor Castle.

SONG,—"IT IS NOT ON THE BATTLE FIELD," &C.

DOORS TO BE OPEN AT 7 O'CLOCK, AND BEGIN AT 8 PRECISELY.

Tickets 2s. each, to be had at J. Munro's, Bookseller, at the Crown Inn, and at Mr. Thos. Smith's.

1830 Political printing: song sheet. Printed by J. Loder.
219×218 mm.

1832 Election notice. Printed by Jackson, Ipswich.
247×200 mm.

1832 Woodbridge Festival notice. Printed by J. Munro.
300×190 mm.

1832 Election notice.
276×224 mm.

A

NEW SONG

TO AN OLD TUNE.

WHY Boys! what's the matter? why all this ado?

Are ye mad to kick up such a hullabaloo?—

Will breaking machinery make the mill go?—

Or burning your corn fill your bellies!—Oh no!

Though the times are but bad, you will render them worse

By refusing to work, you but cut your own purse.

Home, home, Boys! and mind your own business, for shame!

Take care of your household, and likewise your fame—

Leave Frenchmen to brag, of their tri-coloured flag—

We'll boast of our Laws, of our Church, and our King,

Support them all three, and arm against SWING—

Hurrah for the King, the Church, and the State.

RUSHMERE HEATH, SUFFOLK,
December 6, 1830.

J. LODER, Printer, Woodbridge.

Woodbridge
FESTIVAL,

FRIDAY JULY 13, 1832,

TO CELEBRATE THE PASSING OF THE

REFORM BILL.

THE Bells will commence Ringing at 6 o'Clock.

At 12 o'Clock the Presidents, Vice Presidents, Waiters, Band and other attendants will meet before Mr. Grimwood's House, and proceed thence with the Banners and Flags by the Stone Street to the Dinner Tables, in order to place the Banners.

At 1 o'Clock the Band and Constables will dine, and at 2 o'Clock the aged and infirm poor will receive their Dinners and Beer, on sending to Mr. Westhorp's House.

At half past 3 o'Clock the Presidents, Vice Presidents and Waiters, with a sufficient number of men to convey the Dinners from the places where cooked will attend there, and the men and Waiters will remove the Dinners and place them on the Tables, under the superintendance of the Presidents and Vice Presidents, at 4 o'Clock precisely.

The Dinner will commence at 4 o'Clock, immediately after Grace is said by the Grand President and the Signal given by Trumpet.

The Band will play during Dinner.

Immediately after the first supply of Beer has been drank; the Presidents, Vice Presidents and Waiters (leaving, the Constables and one waiter for each table) will with the Band and such of the Men and Boys attend the Dinner as choose to do so; join in a procession with the Flags and Banners through the Town, passing over the Market-Hill, and proceeding down New Street and by the Thoroughfare to the corner of Col. White's residence. Then return to the Crown and passing along through the Quay Lane, and Brewer's Lane, to the Cherry Tree, and afterwards return through Cumberland Street and up Stone Street to the Hill, and should there be sufficient time the procession will afterwards pass through Theatre street, Pound street, and return by well Street to the Tables.

On returning, the Strong Beer will be drawn, and at 9 o'Clock, the Presidents, Vice Presidents, Waiters and Company will join in procession with the Band to the Cricket Ground, for the Exhibition of Fire Works.

.·. *The Inhabitants are particularly requested to close their Shops at 12 o'Clock.*

☞ *No Fire Works will be allowed in any part of the Town.*

The Presidents, Vice Presidents, and other Friends of Reform propose dining together at the Shire-Hall, Woodbridge, on Friday, the 20th inst. at 4 o'Clock. Tickets including a pint of Wine ... each to be had of Mr. Munro and at the Bull Cock and Pie, and White Horse, Inns.

THE FRIENDS

AND

SUPPORTERS

OF

Lord HENNIKER

ARE REQUESTED

TO MEET

AT THE

One-mile Stone

ON THE

WHITTON ROAD

TO-MORROW (THURSDAY,)

AT ONE O'CLOCK PRECISELY.

Committee Room, 20th Dec. 1832.

JACKSON, PRINTER, IPSWICH.

BLUES,

Answer the following

QUESTIONS

BEFORE YOU STIGMATIZE

The Yellows

AS THE

SUPPORTERS OF POPERY.

Who restored the POPE after Buonaparte had dethroned him?

Who restored that devoted tool of the Pope, FERDINAND, and the Inquisition of Spain, and prevented the establishment of a Free Constitutional Government?

And as you *affect* to dread the introduction of Popery into Ipswich, you are asked,—

Who purchased the ground on which the *Roman Catholic Chapel* in Ipswich stands?

Who are the Trustees of that Chapel?

Who assisted in laying the foundation of that Chapel?

Who superintended the building in the absence of the priest?

Col. E——r, his Wife & Family, the Rev. T. C——d, and Mr. Rick. P——r, are referred to for Answers to the four last Questions.

THEATRE, WOODBRIDGE.

On SATURDAY, February 21, 1835,

BY DESIRE OF

Mr. PECKSTON,

PROPRIETOR OF THE WOODBRIDGE GAS WORKS.

The Gas will this Evening be introduced into the Theatre.

The new and popular Comedy, (never acted here,) called The

Climbing Boy;

Or, The Hypocrite Unmasked.

Mr. Strawbery, Mr. FISHER—Sir Gilbert Thorncliffe, Mr. RAY
Jacob Buzzard, Mr. J. FISHER—The Climbing Boy, Master F. FISHER
Jack Ragg, Mr. C. FISHER—Mr. Mordaunt, Mr. WALLACK
Controll, Mr. TWIDDY—Slinker, Mr. HARGRAVE
Chiffionier, Mr. HOLLIDAY—Servants, Poachers, Policeman, &c.

Miss Prudence Strawbery, Mrs. HODGSON—Rebecca, Mrs. FISHER
Rosalie, Miss HAYES—Lucy, Miss MORGAN

A COMIC SONG, by Mr. C. FISHER.

A SONG, BY MISS MORGAN.

After which, (for the only time,) the celebrated Nautical Drama, of The

PILOT;

OR, A STORM AT SEA.

Pilot, Mr. HARGRAVE—Barnstable, Mr. FISHER
Captain Boroughcliff (a regular Yankee,) Mr. RAY
Long Tom Coffin, Mr. C. FISHER—Colonel Howard, Mr. TWIDDY
Serjeant Drill, Master F. FISHER—Lieutenant Griffith, Mr. BOUCHIER,
(being his first appearance in this Company)
Master Merry, Mr. HOLLIDAY—Officer, Mr. WALLACK
Kate Plowden, Miss HAYES—Cecilia, Miss MORGAN
Irishwoman, Mrs. HODGSON

In the course of the Piece the following Scenery and Incidents:
ACT I.
VIEW ON THE SEA COAST.
STORM AT SEA.
Perilous Situation of the Ariel.
RESCUE FROM SHIPWRECK.
ACT II.
SCENE BETWEEN DECKS.
VIEW ON THE SEA COAST.
ACT III.
MARINE VIEW.
COMBAT WITH LONG TOM COFFIN AND
AMERICAN SOLDIERS.
ACT IV.
DECK OF THE ALACRITY.
Barnstable's Rescue From Execution.

GOD SAVE THE QUEEN !!!

When **VICTORIA** donn'd her Crown,
  Not two short years ago ;
Scarce a City or a Town---
  Truer Loyalty could show !
But now that our Young QUEEN
  Is to Hymen's Altar bound,
Our Loyalty---I ween,
  But evaporates IN SOUND !
Victoria has her Mate,
  And old Gipping's Banks are gay ;
E'en Stowmarket has its Fete,
  But for WOODBRIDGE---Well a day !
What a sorry tale it tells
  For the Altar and the Throne ;
When by jangling a few Bells
  All our Loyalty is shown !
The least we could have done,
  Our consistency to seal,
Would have been, in mournful fun,
To have RUNG HER A DUMB PEAL !!

ICHABOD.

WOODBRIDGE,
  Feb. 10th, 1840.

J. MUNRO, PRINTER.

1856 Property notice. Printed by J. Loder.
224 × 287 mm.

1859 Charity notice. Printed by J. Loder.
225 × 277 mm.

1878 Property notice. Printed by J. Loder.
222 × 280 mm.

NOTICE.

HAVING received a Requisition numerously and respectably signed, requesting us to call a General Meeting of the Inhabitants, to consider what steps are necessary to take relative to certain Property now known as the Lime Kiln Quay, in which the Parish is interested, we hereby convene a

PUBLIC MEETING,

AT THE

TOWN HALL,

On WEDNESDAY next, Oct. 15, 1856,

AT TEN O'CLOCK PUNCTUALLY.

G. E. THOMPSON
H. EDWARDS, Jun. } Churchwardens.

WOODBRIDGE, October 11, 1856.   [J. LODER, Printer and Bookseller.]

To celebrate the Royal Visit in 1873 500 loaves of bread and 500 packets of tea were given away to poor persons in Woodbridge Town Hall by the Church Wardens. The Band of the 3rd Suffolk Rifles played on Market Hill. It seems a small thing to have been made so much of !

In the following summer, the Great Eastern Railway printed a bill listing cheap excursion trains from Woodbridge to Yarmouth for the Yarmouth Regatta. The Vestry, or at least the churchwardens or the parish officers, called meetings to discuss Lime Kiln Quay (why, they do not say), to talk about the management of a local charity and finally to purchase part of a property to widen a pavement.

SEKFORD Hospital, WOODBRIDGE.

THE Solicitor of Her Majesty's Attorney General having transmitted for the perusal of the Inhabitants of WOODBRIDGE, the Draft of the proposed Scheme for the future management of this Charity:

NOTICE IS HEREBY GIVEN,

That the same has been deposited at Mr. WOOD's Office, in Church Street, where it may be inspected by the Inhabitants, on any day between the hours of **9** and **6** o'clock.

WOODBRIDGE, June 22, 1859.   **GEORGE GALL**
DAVY CROWE } Churchwardens.

J. LODER, PRINTER AND BOOKSELLER.

NOTICE

IN PURSUANCE OF A REQUEST

A MEETING

OF THE

RATE-PAYERS OF WOODBRIDGE

Will be held in the TOWN HALL, in Woodbridge aforesaid, On WEDNESDAY, the 22nd inst. at 10 o'clock, a.m. for the purpose of considering the advisability of purchasing a portion of the property in the Thoroughfare, late belonging to and occupied by Mr. Giles, and now the property of Mr. B. D. Gall, and unoccupied, situated between the Savings Bank and the Road leading to Doric Place, with a view to improving the pavement at that part of the street.

WOODBRIDGE,
May 17, 1878.   **T. CARTHEW**
A. S. GROSS } Churchwardens.

J. LODER, PRINTER AND STATIONER, WOODBRIDGE.

1874 Railway Excursion notice. Printed at the Great Eastern
Railway Company's works, Stratford.
210×140 mm.

GREAT EASTERN RAILWAY.

YARMOUTH

REGATTA,

TUESDAY, 11th AUGUST, 1874.

ON THE ABOVE DATE,

CHEAP EXCURSION TICKETS

WILL BE ISSUED TO

YARMOUTH

AS UNDER :—

FROM	TRAINS AT		Fares to Yarmouth & back.		
	morn.	even.	1st Class. s. d.	2nd Class. s. d.	3rd Class. s. d.
Ipswich	7 10	11 26			
Bealings	7 29	11 46			
Woodbridge..............	7 38	11 55			
Melton	7 43	12 0	6 0	4 6	3 0
Framlingham	6 50	11 40			
Parham	6 57	11 46			
Marlesford	7 5	11 53			
Wickham Market	7 54	12 10			
Saxmundham	8 9	12 45	4 0	3 0	2 6
Darsham	8 19	12 55			
Halesworth	8 32	1 7	3 6	2 6	1 6
Brampton...............	8 41	1 16			
Beccles..................	8 57	1 30	2 0	1 6	1 0
Yarmouth ....arr.	9 35	2 5			

Returning from Yarmouth at 6 15 p.m. the same day.

S. SWARBRICK,
General Manager.

London, August, 1874.

PRINTED AT THE COMPANY'S WORKS, STRATFORD.

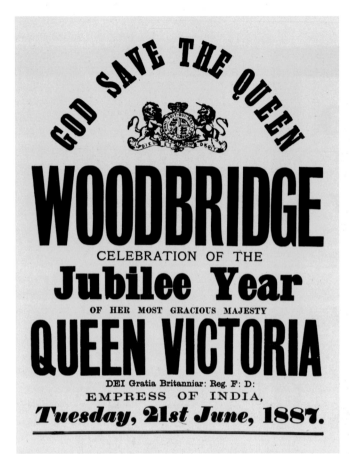

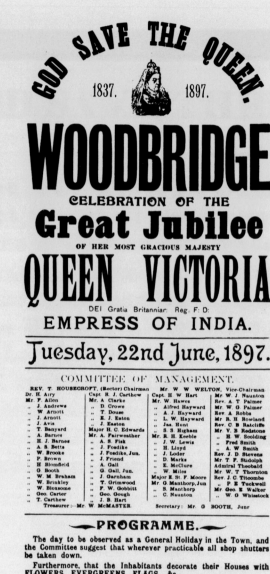

In 1887 Queen Victoria's Jubilee was celebrated with a day of processions, a regatta, a promenade concert and a display of fireworks, and the annual regatta was announced in red and old gold on black paper. In 1893 Woodbridge was celebrating again. It was for the marriage of the Duke of York to Princess May (afterwards respectively King George V and Queen Mary). For this occasion a 'Torchlight Masquerade' was announced on another handsome poster again printed by Mr Booth in red and old gold on a black background. Four years later Woodbridge was still celebrating; this time it was for the old Queen's Diamond Jubilee and the celebrations were advertised on a poster 29 inches (743 mm) long! And so, as far as Woodbridge was concerned, the century came peacefully to its end.

This picture of Woodbridge in the nineteenth century has shown something of the reactions of a small East Anglian town to national events. East Anglia was then, and to some extent still is, an agricultural backwater. Woodbridge served the import and export needs of this farming community. The industrial revolution had little effect on it, at least until the arrival of the railway in 1856. The notice at the top of page 110, dated 15 October 1856, must have referred to the East Suffolk Railway Company's purchase of the land by Lime Kiln Quay, on which they built Woodbridge station. The little port still prospered until the turn of the century, when the combination of railway and road transport finally killed it.

1887 Regatta poster. Printed by G. Booth.
525×255 mm.

1893 Marriage Celebrations poster. Printed by G. Booth.
635×254 mm.

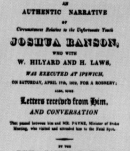

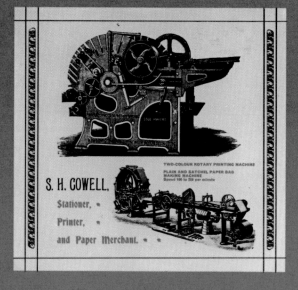

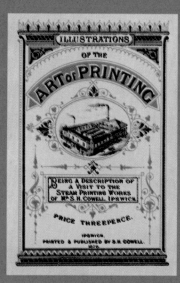

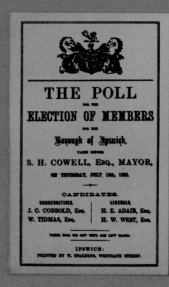

1968 Printer's Ephemera calendar. Printed by W. S. Cowell Ltd.
450×292 mm.

The roots of such English towns as Woodbridge lie deep in the past. The bill about the management of the Seckford Hospital on the same page is in reference to a charity endowed by an Elizabethan courtier called Thomas Seckford. By 1861 the endowment had grown to a size whereby the Governors could build a fine new row of almshouses.

In the 1800s farming was a prosperous industry. East Anglia, as the 'Grain State' of England, reflected this by the number of fine farm houses and small manors that were built or rebuilt in those years. All this was to change with the repeal of the Corn Laws in 1846. The introduction of cheap foreign grain soon brought down the price of bread and caused a depression in the farming industry. Woodbridge reflected all these changes. One could well have produced a pictorial *Akenfield** by means of auction notices of bankrupt farms, posters for the apprehension of out-of-work farm workers who had been caught poaching, and so on.

Woodbridge produced only one celebrity in the nineteenth century and that was an eccentric called Edward Fitzgerald (1809–1893), the translator of *The Rubaiyat of Omar Khayyam,* first published in 1859.

As for this printed ephemera, small hand-press printers like Loder or Booth continued to produce posters and bills for the day to day business of the town. The needs of larger, more industrialized centres demanded more sophisticated kinds of printing. The steam printer came into being. One such firm was Cowells of Ipswich.

Ipswich, the county town of Suffolk, is only some eight miles from Woodbridge. In 1818 A. K. Cowell a corn merchant of St Clements, set up his second son in a stationery and printing business. His earliest known piece of printed ephemera was a little sixteen page octavo booklet, entitled *Narrative of Circumstances relative to the unfortunate youth, Joshua Ranson, executed at Ipswich on 17 April 1819.* This dire penalty was for stealing four silver spoons after a drunken frolic.

One hundred and fifty years after Samuel Harrison Cowell started printing, the firm celebrated the anniversary by publishing a calendar, with a design made up from various pieces of ephemera from their archives including the Joshua Ranson booklet. Among the other pieces were an invitation in 1879 to the firm's 'Annual Wayzgoose', tobacco labels for local firms, a series of increasingly severe demands for payment and a small printed notice of 1831 announcing that the firm was in the wine and spirit business, as well as printing. They were offering good cordial gin at eight shillings and sixpence per gallon! This was probably printed on the Imperial press shown at the bottom of the page.

Printed ephemera used in this manner for backing up the story of a particular business can often provide pointed, even witty, comment to accounts that only too often are complaisant and dull.

Akenfield: Portrait of an English Village. Ronald Blythe. Allen Lane: The Penguin Press. 1969

7. Hartlepool: A coal port in the nineteenth century

Any attempt to reveal something of the past social history of a place by the use of printed ephemera does, of course, depend on the availability of material. The story of Hartlepool is here told in posters, notices and billheads, from the spike files of John Procter, who set up a print shop in the town in 1834. These files were rescued a dozen years or so ago by Mr Robert Wood, a social historian and the headmaster of one of Hartlepool's schools. The appalling condition of these files, which were well over a hundred years old, and how Mr Wood cleaned them, is described in the next chapter.

There are other comparable collections, that deal with the life of one town, such as Mr George Arnott's collections of Woodbridge ephemera and the printer John Soulby's files and guardbooks of Ulverston, which are preserved in the public library at nearby Barrow-in-Furness and at the Museum of Rural Life, Reading. Mr Wood's collection is unique in that it spans the nineteenth-century growth of a new coal port and parallels the growth of the railways.

The work of such tradesmen as John Procter goes unsung, yet printers like this were often key figures in growing industrial communities. Printing was cheap and anyone with a grievance, a political bias or something to sell made use of the printer's services. Nothing of any importance could have happened in Hartlepool without John Procter knowing about it.

When he set up his press he had no opposition and by the time other printers were working in the town they provided little competition. Procter must have been a good and reliable businessman and he was an excellent craftsman, making the most lively use of the display typefaces from Thorowgood's and Figgins's and Caslon's foundries.

Auction sales, billheads, tickets and notices for the Hartlepool Dock and Railway Company, coal certificates, notices of every arrival of a new cargo and of every shipwreck, of every visit of a strolling player or lecturer with a diorama, came off John Procter's press. In addition to this he acted as an agent for the players and lecturers. As Robert Wood has written: 'He was a most methodical man. He kept all his correspondence, and the survival of these tattered and grimy spike files, some a hundred and thirty years old, enables us to fill in the background to the bills he printed.'*

In the time of the Prince Regent, Hartlepool was a quiet little fishing village, set in the midst of good farming country, on the headland sheltering Hartlepool Bay just north of the river Tees, yet it was within a few miles of the Durham coalfields. All the coal that went to London was exported from the Tyne and Wear, but in 1825 this monopoly came to an end. In that year the Stockton and Darlington Railway was opened, with horses drawing the wagons, except for their one solitary steam engine. Because of the short haul, within three days of the railway opening the price of coal was halved and Stockton's

* *Victorian Delights*. Robert Wood. Evans Brothers, London 1967.

STOCKTON & DARLINGTON
RAILWAY.

The Public are respectfully informed that the

RAILWAY
COACH
BETWEEN
SAINT HELEN'S AUCKLAND & SHILDON,

Will commence to run daily, on Monday, the
10th. of September, 1838, (Sundays excepted)

TWO ADDITIONAL TRIPS

to and from the above places, as under:—

From St. Helen's at 10 o'clock | From Shildon at 11 o'clock.
  do.   do. at 2 do | do.   do. at 3 do.

FARES:—INSIDE 6d.—OUTSIDE 3d.
THE OTHER LONG TRAINS WILL START AS USUAL.

By Order of the Committee,
JOHN GRAHAM, *Inspector.*

NEW SHILDON. September 5th 1838.

P. FAIR, PRINTER AND BOOKBINDER, BISHOP AUCKLAND

success as a port was ensured. But Stockton is some way from the sea. A new coalfield had been opened up in south-east Durham and Hartlepool was nearer to it than either Stockton or Middlesbrough. In 1832 new harbour works were begun and the Hartlepool Railway brought coal wagons to the staithes. Once the harbour had been dredged out, ships could enter port, and load and leave on the same tide.

The Hartlepool Dock and Railway Company charged heavy tolls on the coal brought down by wagons from the mines, but gave the collier brigs cut-rate dues to attract them to the new port. The success of the undertaking was assured. Then came the opposition in the form of the Stockton and Hartlepool Railway which undercut the tolls levied on the Hartlepool Railway and aroused great opposition in the old port. In 1844 an Act was passed, permitting the new railway company to build a new harbour and dock under the name of Hartlepool West Harbour and Dock Company. This was the beginning of West Hartlepool.

Hartlepool must have been a fairly rumbustious town during the building of the new docks. The local fishermen did not appreciate the imported navvies eyeing their girls, though no doubt the navvies had good cause to stare at the bonnie lasses, who went shrimping with their petticoats hoisted high above their knees.

Ship-building was started in Hartlepool in 1837 and at West Hartlepool in the 1850s. The first ship built in the new town was the *Mirage*, a fast tea clipper. She was built of wood and launched in 1854. A year later her builder, John Pile, launched his first iron-built steamer, the *Demetrius*.

In those days most Hartlepool tradesmen had shares in individual ships and even in the small local shipping companies. If their ships prospered it was an easy transition from grocer's shop to shipyard. For instance, Thomas Furness, a prosperous wholesale provision merchant, was persuaded by his younger brother Christopher to buy a ship to carry their goods to the Continent. Christopher Furness, seeing the possibilities that shipping offered, joined the ship-building firm of Withy's when Edward Withy migrated to New Zealand because he was disgusted at the high rate of income tax! Christopher Furness with Henry Withy together formed the world famous shipping firm of Furness Withy and ended his life as Lord Grantley.

As the ship-building industry in Hartlepool prospered, engineering works grew up alongside the docks to serve the industry's needs and also to build locomotives and steam engines, boilers, cranes and rolling stock.

Timber was imported for pit props and for house and ship-building. Canvas mills and ropewalks came into being to meet the still considerable needs of sailing ships. Shipping, ship-building and the export of coal were the mainstays of West Hartlepool's fortunes throughout the nineteenth century.

1834 Freight receipt.
120×190 mm.

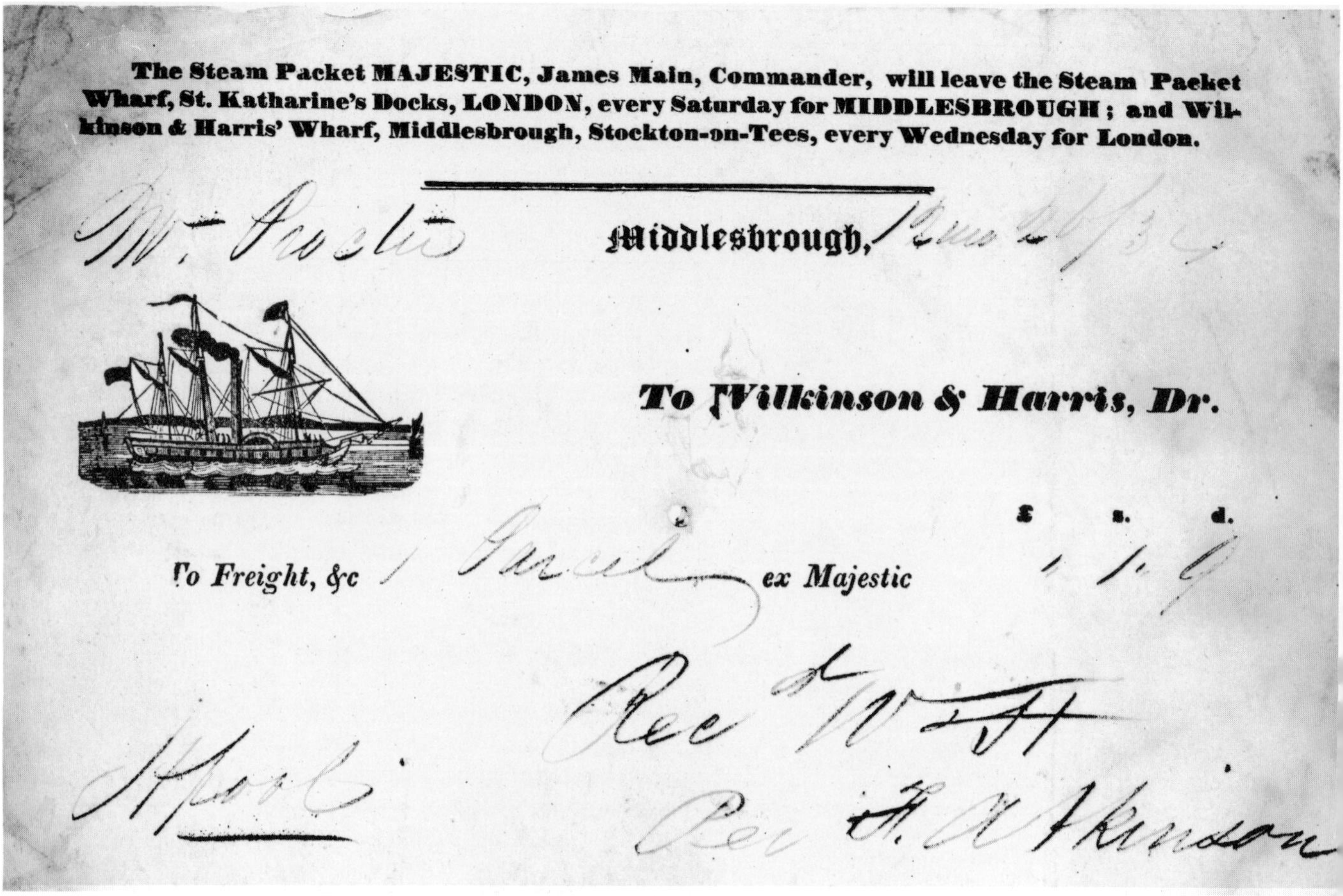

The Steam Packet **MAJESTIC**, James Main, Commander, will leave the Steam Packet Wharf, St. Katharine's Docks, **LONDON**, every Saturday for **MIDDLESBROUGH**; and Wilkinson & Harris' Wharf, Middlesbrough, Stockton-on-Tees, every Wednesday for London.

Middlesbrough,

To Wilkinson & Harris, Dr.

To Freight, &c   ex Majestic

Yet with all this activity there were few records kept. The lists of ships built were so inadequate that it was not until Mr Robert Wood found a series of narrow paper streamers that anything like a complete list of ships built in one particular shipyard could be compiled. These streamers had the names of vessels and their launching dates printed on them. They were the proofs for the gold-printed satin ribbons that were tied round the traditional bouquet of flowers that would be handed to whoever was performing the launching ceremony.

One can get a series of impressions of Hartlepool viewed mostly from the sea, from the copper engravings that decorated some of the coal certificates issued by the local coal fitters. These certificates were to do with cargoes of coals from the various local collieries. One of these engravings is of a brig close-hauled with a paddle tug ahead of her; another is of the light on the jetty and one which is signed 'Thorpe del & Jordison sc' is of the inner basin. There is also a panoramic view of Castle Eden Colliery signed 'Lamberts'. Another view from the sea with a brig hove to in the foreground is from a leaflet printed in German and describing the port of Hartlepool. It was issued by John Pace & Co, shipping agents.

Other ship's manifests are decorated with cuts of collier brigs and full-rigged ships and various kinds of loco

c. 1840. Views of Hartlepool from shipping agents leaflet and coal certificates from local collieries. 221 mm wide.

Note: all the Hartlepool printing comes from the files of J. Procter.

motives. Incidentally these manifests are pleasant pieces of typography, with discreet use of heavy black letter (gothic), bold Egyptian and decorated Tuscan typefaces.

c. 1840 Coal certificate incorporating a collier brig. Proof.
150×270 mm.

c. 1840 Coal certificate. The cut shows Sharp's Standard
Passenger Engine (1837). Revised proof.
145×272 mm.

c. 1840 Coal certificate. Proof.
145×272 mm.

TONS_____ MEN
CLEARED FOR_____

Hartlepool,_____ 184_

I have shipped on board the_____ of_____

Mr._____ Master,

_____ Tons & _____ Cwts of

THOMAS RICHMUND GALE BRADDYLL, ESQ. & PARTNERS'

East Hetton Double Screened Small Coals,

(One half of the above-named quantity being wrought and gotten out of Kelloe Colliery, and the remaining one half out of Garmondsway Moor Colliery.)

TONS   MEN FOR

Hartlepool,_____ 184_
Port of Stockton.

I have Shipped on board the_____

of_____ Master

_____ Tons of

THE CASSOP COAL COMPANY'S

Hartlepool Wallsend Coals. from Cassop Colliery

Hartlepool,_____ 184_
Port of Stockton.

I have Shipped on board the_____

of_____ Master

_____ Tons of

The Right Honble. Lord Howden & Partners'

NUT COALS

At_____ Shillings and Sixpence per Chaldron of 53 Cwt.

CUSTOM HOUSE, HARTLEPOOL.

_____ P. C. Officer.

118

c. 1840 Coal certificate. The engraving is by Lamberts.
136×260 mm.

1850 Advertisement leaflet: coal. Printed by Annett, Fareham.
101×163 mm.

1840 Coal certificate. Proof.
137×253 mm.

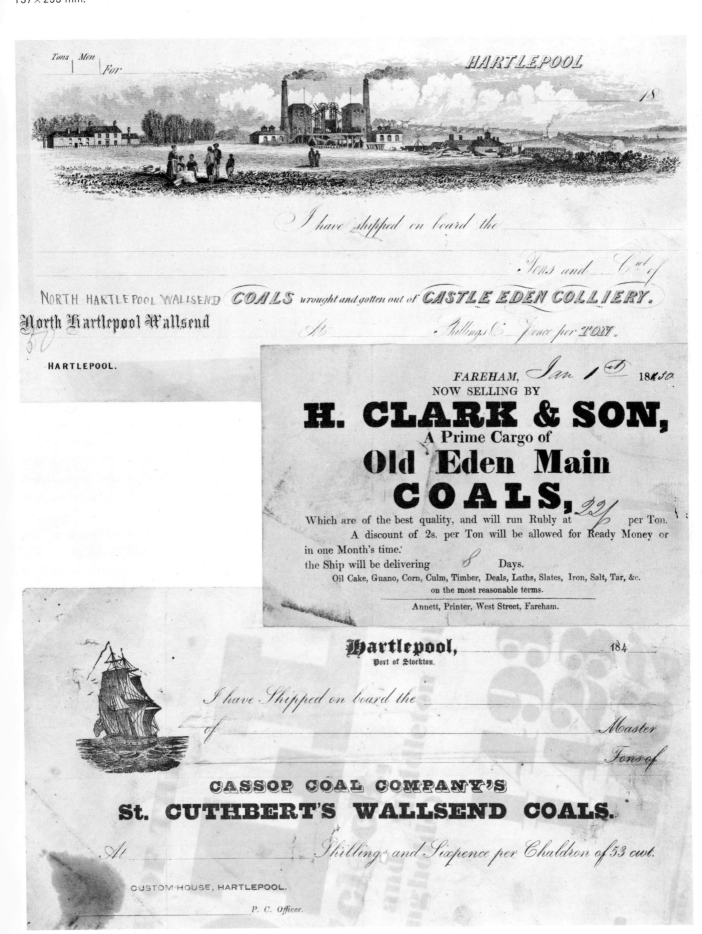

M. MEEK,

Most respectfully begs leave to return his sincere thanks to those Families who have kindly given him a share of their Patronage and support during the short period he has been employed as **Agent to the East India Tea Company;** and at the same time he begs to inform his Friends and the Public, that in addition to the above Agency, he has commenced the **GROCERY BUSINESS**, and hopes by offering genuine Articles, to merit a continuance of those favours hitherto bestowed upon him; assuring all who may kindly give him a share of their custom, that he will most assiduously endeavour to give the greatest satisfaction.

The following is a List of his Prices.

TEAS.	s.	d.	COFFEES.	s.	d.
Imperial Gunpowder Tea	7	0	Common	1	4
Good do.	6	0	Ceylon	1	6
Young Hyson	6	0	Good	1	8
Good Green	5	0	Java	1	10
Common	4	0	Mocha	2	0
BLACK TEAS.			**Good Raw Sugars.**		
Howqua	6	0	Good Brown	0	6½
Souchong	6	0	Refined	0	7½
Rough and Strong	5	0	Do. Crystalized	0	8
Good Breakfast Tea	4	0	Grey's Genuine Tobacco 11½ per qr. lb.		

And other Articles equally cheap in the Grocery line.

M. Meek, begs to call the attention of Sailors and others, to his well made stock of Seamens Clothing, which he begs to offer at reduced prices.

Ships also supplied with Bonded Stores.

J. Procie, Printer, Union Place, High Street Hartlepool.

Of the trade of the town in the 1830s, Mr Meek, agent to the East India Tea Company, announces he has set up as a grocer. Thomas Young, another grocer, says in 1846 he can undercut any one else's prices and he also sells Spencer's Genuine Unadulterated Shag and Best Dantzig Black Beer. The auctioneers in Hartlepool seemed to have had a busy time selling off stocks of clothes, hats and caps and drapery with a marvellous list of picturesquely sounding materials.

As many of the types of material mentioned in these bills are now obsolete a brief description might help the reader to visualize them.

Broadcloth: a fine plain woven double-width cloth used mainly for men's clothes.

Cassimere (cashmere): a thin fine twilled woollen cloth.

Kersey: a kind of coarse ribbed woollen cloth, originally from Kersey in Suffolk.

Petersham: formerly a heavy cloth suitable for the making of overcoats.

Moleskin: a strong soft fine-piled cotton fustian the surface of which was shaved before dyeing. Trousers were often made of moleskin.

Fustain (fustian): a coarse cloth made of cotton and flax. The name derives from Fostat, a suburb of Cairo, whence the stuff first came.

Cross-over: a fabric having the design running across from selvedge to selvedge.

Merino: a soft woollen material like French cashmere, originally made from the wool of the Merino sheep.

Bombasin (bombasine): a twilled dress fabric made of cotton and worsted or silk and worsted. It was often dyed black and used for mourning clothes.

Lutestring: a kind of glossy silk fabric.

Bobbin net: a machine made cotton net.

Swansdown: a soft thick closely woven woollen cloth or thick cotton cloth with a nap on one side.

Toilanet (toilinet): a kind of fine woollen cloth formerly used for waistcoats for grooms, huntsmen etc.

Valencia: a mixed fabric for waistcoats having a wool weft with a warp of silk, cotton or linen and usually striped.

The trade of a coal port like this followed certain seasonal patterns. In the autumn and winter potatoes from Norway are on sale on the dockside next door to Mr Hills the block-maker and apples from Hamburg are to be auctioned as soon as they arrive. Amongst the bucolic imports was a cargo of 28 tons of Norfolk hay, brought by the brig *Ocean.*

This brig belonged to Kings Lynn. A contemporary account book from Blumer's Shipyard has an entry that the *Ocean* had made use of their hard to have her bottom scrubbed and had bought six gallons of coal tar at sixpence a gallon and 63 lbs of black lead at four and a half pence per pound. An indication of the extent of coastal trade between Hartlepool and East Anglia is that the same yard had as customers the *Blakeney Packet,* a sloop from

1843 Auctioneer's notice: Apples.
192×220 mm.

c. 1844 Hatter's notice.
222×185 mm.

1843 Announcement: baker.
192×225 mm.

1846 Auctioneer's notice: Norwegian potatoes.
190×229 mm.

MR. HENRY LAYBOURN

Begs to inform his Friends and the Public generally,
that he his

Daily Expecting

AConsignment

OF

APPLES,

BY THE "PILOT," CAPT. GOLDSACK,

FROM HAMBURG,

Which he his instructed to sell

BY PUBLIC AUCTION ON ARRIVAL.

☞ *Particulars will be given in future Bills.*

Hartlepool, 17th October, 1843.

J. PROCTER, PRINTER, UNION PLACE, HARTLEPOOL.

ANN STUART,

BREAD & BISCUIT

BAKER,

Returns her sincere thanks to her Friends and the
Public generally of Hartlepool and the Neighbourhood for the support she has received during the 10
years she has been in business, and respectfully begs
to acquaint them that she has removed from High
Street into Cleveland Street, where she is now carrying on the above business in its various branches; and
she hopes by vending an article of superior quality
at a moderate rate of profit, to ensure a continuance
of their favours.

Shipping supplied with Bread and Biscuits on liberal Terms.

Cleveland Street, Hartlepool, August 14th 1843.

From J. Procter's Office, High Street, Hartlepool.

VICTORIA HOUSE.

HATS & CAPS.

Those who admire good-formed Hats and Caps of first-rate quality, at the lowest price
possible, will find the largest assortment in upwards of one hundred different Shapes at

POTTER'S

THE CELEBRATED HAIR CUTTER,

NORTHGATE, HARTLEPOOL,

Who is appointed Agent for some of the first Establishments in London, from which he
continues to receive a fresh supply every month

HATS.	s.	d	CAPS.	s.	d
Rustic Billys	1	0	Lawn Forages	1	0
Covered do.	1	3	Locomotive Caps	1	6
Japanned	3	6	Railway do.	1	9
Gossamer	3	6	Seal do.	2	0
Men's Waterproof	4	6	Travelling do.	2	6
Excellent quality	5	6	Calf Skins	3	0
Beautiful Silk	6	6	Fitch do	3	0
Superior do.	7	6	Mich do.	3	3
Splendid do.	8	6	Plush Caps	4	6
Superior Shortnap	10	6	Sable	7	6
Good Stuff	12	6	Canadian	8	6
Superior do.	16	6	Astrachan	18	6
Very best	20	0	Cloth Caps from 6d. upwards.		

BOY'S HATS AND CAPS IN GREAT VARIETY.

LADIES', GIRL'S, & CHILDREN'S BEAVER BONNETS.

CAUTION. Victoria House is immediately opposite Mr. R. Humble's, Cleveland Arms.

FROM J. PROCTER'S OFFICE, HIGH STREET, HARTLEPOOL.

ON SALE,

In the Warehouse, on the Victoria Dock Side,

NEXT DOOR TO Mr. HILL'S, BLOCK MAKER,

A QUANTITY OF EXCELLENT NORWEGIAN

POTATOES

At 2s. per Bushel,

WEIGHING SIX STONE TO THE BUSHEL.

APPLY AT THE WAREHOUSE.

Hartlepool, Dec. 28th, 1846.

Printed by J. PROCTER, Hartlepool.

Maldon, the brig *William Chapman* of Colchester, the *Hop*
of Lynn, the *Royal Adelaide* of Colchester and also from th
same port the *Volunteer*, the *Venus* and the *Jessie Brown*
There were also the *Cognac Packet* of Harwich, the bri
Malta of Ipswich, the schooner *Jane* of Aldboro' an
various other vessels.

One little printed notice of the sale of a cargo of ha
resulted in this digression. These ephemeral pieces o
printed paper provide the props and framework for a stor
and lead one in many directions. It is a form of researc
where the observant eye is as important as patien
scholarship. Now to return to Hartlepool's High Street.

FOR SALE,

IN THE

HARTLEPOOL DOCKS,

A CARGO OF

ABOUT 28 TONS

OF

FINE NORFOLK

HAY,

PER BRIG "OCEAN,"

CAPTAIN HILL.

For further Particulars, as to Price, Sample, &c.,
apply to

SHERINTON FOSTER,

Ship Broker, Town Wall, Hartlepool.

J. PROCTER, PRINTER, HARTLEPOOL.

1837 Auction notice: drapery.
282×225 mm.

1837 Auction notice: clothes.
143×225 mm.

1841 Auction notice: headgear.
282×225 mm.

1841 Announcement: shoe shop. Uncorrected proof.
287×221 mm.

TO BE SOLD

BY AUCTION

On Monday, Tuesday, 1st. 2nd. and following Days, May, 1837,

THE WHOLE OF THE

Valuable Stock of Linen & Woollen

Drapery,

BELONGING TO

R. FRANCE,

High Street, Hartlepool,

Who is about leaving the Town;

CONSISTING OF

Broad and Narrow Cloths, Cassimeres, Kerseys, and Petershams; Waistcoatings of every description; Beveteens, Moleskins, Fustains, and Cotton Cords; Home-made & Irish Linens; Checks, Ginghams, and Cross-overs; Flannels and Kerseys; 7—8 and Ell-wide Printed Calicos, do. Muslins; 3—4 & 6—4 Black & Coloured Merinos; black Bombasins and Lutestrings; Silk and Cotton Shawls; Silk & Cotton Handkerchiefs; 4—4 Bobbin Nets; do. Quilling Edgings and Lace; Gloves; Hosiery of every kind; a large assortment of

WATERPROOF HATS,

Boy's Caps, and a variety of other Articles too numerous to mention.

SALE TO COMMENCE EACH DAY AT 1 O'CLOCK.

Mr. MERRYWEATHER, Auctioneer.

J. Procter, Printer, Hartlepool.

HARTLEPOOL.

To be Sold by Auction,

IN THE MARKET-PLACE, HARTLEPOOL,

On Saturday, the 18th March, 1837,

BY MR. WM. MERRYWEATHER,

A LARGE QUANTITY OF READY MADE

Clothes,

Consisting of Woollen Cloth and Fustain Coats and Fustain Top Jackets; do. do. Trousers; Toilanet and Swansdown Waistcoats; Boy's Cloth and Leather Caps; Men and Boy's Silk and Wool Hats; Straw Bonnets; Men's Cloth and Fustain Gaiters; Striped Shirts; Flannel and Cotton Drawers; Neck and Pocket Handkerchiefs, and various other Articles.

THE SALE TO BEGIN AT THREE IN THE AFTERNOON.

J. Procter, Printer, High Street, Hartlepool.

In 1837 Mr R. France, Linen and Woollen Draper, is selling up his stock, because 'he is about leaving the town'. He does not say why! His troubles must have blown over, for a year later he returns from visiting the 'Principal Manufacturing Towns' with a new stock of goods at astonishingly low prices.

Boot and shoe makers and bakers vie with manufacturers of ornamental chimney tops and watch, clock and compass makers. Mr G. Wright, a lemonade merchant, tells his public he is now licensed to sell game and Mr J.

HARTLEPOOL.

To be Sold

BY AUCTION,

BY MR. HENRY LAYBOURN,

On Saturday the 6th Day Feb. 1841,

ON THE PREMISES LATELY OCCUPIED BY

Mr Whaley, Watch-maker,

Market Place,

A QUANTITY OF

HATS

And CAPS

Of various sizes and qualities.

THE SALE TO COMMENCE AT ONE O'CLOCK.

J. PROCTER, PRINTER, HARTLEPOOL.

NEW

Boot & Shoe

SHOP,

CORNER OF CLEVELAND STREET, NORTHGATE,

Hartlepool.

C. HARDY,

BOOT & SHOE MAKER,

Begs most respectfully to inform the Inhabitants of Hartlepool and its Vicinity, that he has Commenced business in the above Shop, where he hopes by reasonable Terms and perseving attention, to give satisfaction to those who may please to favour him with their Commands.

A choice assortment of

Boots & Shoes

Constantly on hand.

ORDERS EXECUTED WITH NEATNESS & DESPATCH.

8th March, 1841.

J. PROCTER, PRINTER, HARTLEPOOL.

A GREAT SAVING by PUR-CHASING GOODS of

R. France,

Linen and Woollen

DRAPER,

Haberdasher, Hosier, Hatter, &c.

HIGH STREET,

HARTLEPOOL.

R. F. has just returned from the Principal Manufacturing Towns, where he has purchased a large and valuable

STOCK OF GOODS

Suitable for the present Season,

CONSISTING OF

**Superfine BROAD WOOLLEN CLOTHS from 5s. 6d. per yard, worth 10s.
Narrow do. 2s. 6d. Cassimeres and Kerseys at**

Astonishingly low prices !!

A great variety of Striped & Checked Buckskins from 2s;

Toilanet, Valencia and Swansdown, WAISTCOATING from 1s. per Waistcoat Breast;

Bath Cords and Cantoons for Gentlemen's Summer Coats and Trousers, at 9d. per yard; Cotton Cords 6d. Flannels 6d. Grey and White Calicoes 2d. yard; Large Cotton Sheets 2s. per pair;

PRINTED MUSLIN DRESSES AT HALF THE REGULAR PRICES;

Printed Cambrics at a great reduction; Black & Coloured Lutestrings in great variety; Silk and Cotton

Shawls 20 per cent. below the usual prices;

Ditto Handkerchiefs; Unbleached Cotton Stockings from 5d. per pair; White do. 4½d black & coloured Worsted do. 9d. Gentlemen's black & coloured Silk Stocks 6d. each; Gauze and Bonnet broad Ribbons from 2d. per yard; 4-4 thread Net 3d. per yard; Broad Frilling do. ½d. yard; Lace Caps at 1d. each.

Boy's Cloth Caps 6d. each;

Gentlemen's Beaver Hats 2s. 9d.

And every other Article equally low.

N. B. No connexion with any Shop in Hartlepool, or in Newcastle, the whole of the Stock being direct from the Manufacturer.

July, 1838.

J. PROCTER, PRINTER, HARTLEPOOL.

Ship Materials for Sale.

TobeSold

BY AUCTION,

(Messrs. Sotheran, Auctioneers,)

On Saturday the 26th day of August, 1837,

ON THE DOCK WALLS, AT HARTLEPOOL

3 ANCHORS AND
2 HEMP CABLES.

N. B. The Sale to commence precisely at 1 o'clock.

J. Procter, Printer.

£2 Reward.

Whoever may pick up the Body of **JOSEPH HEPPINSTALL**, who was drowned out of the Sloop, "The William," of Hartlepool, off Flambro' Head, on Wednesday, the 23rd ult., will be rewarded as above, on application to **JOHN SHEPHERD**, Pilot, Hartlepool.

Joseph Heppinstall is a stout-made man and of middle stature, and marked on his right arm in blue ink, **J. H. M. C.**, with an Anchor.

Hartlepool, 1st March, 1848.

Printed by J. PROCTER, Union Place, High Street, Hartlepool.

Procter, the printer of all this material, sets out a list of almanacs, pocket books and tide tables for the year 1844.

Hartlepool's connection with both rail and sea is shown in many bills and notices. There are 'Reward' notices for information about damage to the railway track and for information about the forceful intimidation of the crew of the ship *John White* and for finding the body of a drowned sailor. James and Isaac Thompson, railway carriers, say they will carry goods, grain and furniture at reduced rates. Their leaflet is decorated with a little woodcut of one of Stephenson's engines, drawing a cattle truck and a wagon of mixed merchandise. The Hartlepool Railway inform their public of a change in the times of their trains – their notice decorated with a very archaic cut of a locomotive of no known type and two passenger coaches. Sailing notices offer fast passages in first-class sailing schooners and day trips in powerful steam boats. One of these was to Sunderland to witness 'the removal of the stupendous lighthouse a distance of nearly 50 yards'.

STOCKTON
AND
HARTLEPOOL
RAILWAY.

£5.
REWARD.

WHEREAS

Some evil disposed person has removed and taken away several stakes, or level pegs, and thereby caused much inconvenience and damage to the works on the said Railway.

THIS IS TO GIVE NOTICE,

That the above Reward will be given to any person giving such information as may lead to the apprehension and conviction of the offender.

JOHN FOWLER,
Resident Engineer.

Greatham, Feb. 15th 1840.

From the Office of J. Procter, Hartlepool.

LIST OF
Almanacks and Pocket Books,
FOR THE YEAR, 1844.

J. PROCTER,
BOOKSELLER, STATIONER, PRINTER, ETC., ETC.,
Has just received the following ALMANACKS, &c.,

	s.	d.		s.	d.
Hannay	0	6	British	1	0
Old Moore	0	6	Companion to do.	2	6
Moore improved	0	9	Comic (Tilt's)	2	6
British Farmer	1	0	Oliver and Boyd's	0	3
Clerical	0	9	Poor Richard	0	3
Clergyman	2	6	Medical	1	0
Englishman and Family	1	0	Rees's Diary	0	6
Goldsmith	0	6	Pawsey	0	6
Johnson's Gardner	1	0	Graham's Post-Office Sheet	0	1
Lady's & Gentleman's Diary	1	4	Do. Mounted on Roller	0	6
Mechanic	1	0	Do. Book	0	1
White's Ephemeris	1	0	Prophetic Messenger	2	6
Commercial Sheet	0	6	Diamond	0	1
Gilbert's Vestry Sheet	0	6	Tilt Pocket	0	6
Wing's Sheet	0	6	New Year's Gift	0	1
Stationer's Sheet	2	0	The Original Poor Richard		
Davison's	0	1	with 38 Illustrations	0	1
Moore's Improved Weather	0	1	Wesley	0	1

HOUSEKEEPERS' ACCOUNT BOOKS OF VARIOUS KINDS.

POCKET BOOKS.

	s.	d.		s.	d.
Kearsley's Gentleman's Pocket Ledger	3	6	Poole's Elegant Pocket Album	2	6
Adcock's Engineer	6	0	Do. Gentleman's	2	6
Marshall's Commercial	3	6	New Ladies' Diary	2	6
Do. Gentleman's	2	6	Marshall's Ladies' Elegant Pocket Souvenir	2	6
Carnau's Ladies	2	6	The Ladies' Keepsake	2	6
Poole's Select Pocket Remembrancer	2	6	Ladies' Polite Remembrancer	2	6
Do. London Annual Repository	2	6	Graham's Comic	1	0
Marshall's Ladies' Fashionable Do.	2	6	Do. Ladies' Annual Repository, &c.	1	6

Hartlepool Tide Table 6d. Hoppus's do. 1s. Cooper's do. 6d.
and Harper's 1s.

Printed by J. Procter, Union Office, West End of High Street, Hartlepool.

128

GORLESTON-ON-SEA
"Waiting for the Smacks."

PADDLING AT DUSK.

Little bits of muslin
  Little bits of lace,
Make the streets and sea-shore
    Quite a lovely place.

"One thing leads to another."

"I'm far enough away to feel I want you."

STANDING FOR
THREE DONKEYS

"BY THE BRINY."

PETS OF THE PARADE

"BY THE BRINY."

"IS IT QUITE
SAFE 'ENERY?"

c. 1912 Lithographically printed advertisements and packaging.
237 × 197 mm. (see page 145).

opposite page 12

G. WRIGHT,

Lemonade Manufacturer,

LICENSED

DEALER in GAME,

VICTORIA STREET,

HARTLEPOOL.

Respectfully announces to the Nobility, Clergy, Gentry, and Public
generally of Hartlepool and Neighbourhood, that he has commenced
Selling

GAME
AND
POULTRY

Of every description, and trusts, by keeping a Good Stock constantly
on hand, supplying them at Fair Market Prices, to merit that support
and encouragement it will ever be his study to obtain.

Hartlepool, July 30th, 1851.

From the Office of J. PROCTER, High Street, Hartlepool, and Victoria Terrace, West Hartlepool.

HARTLEPOOL RAILWAY.

The public are informed that an

ALTERATION

Has taken place in the times of Departure of the Passenger Trains of this Railway, which in future will Start

FROM HARTLEPOOL TO CASTLE EDEN, HASWELL, & SUNDERLAND.	FROM HARTLEPOOL TO DURHAM.
In the Morning at quarter before **9**	*In the Morning at quarter before* **9**
Do. quarter past . **11**	*Do. Afternoon* . **4**
Do. Afternoon . . **4**	

On and after Tuesday the 2nd March, the Fares will be raised.

	FIRST CLASS,		SECOND CLASS.	
	s.	*d.*	*s.*	*d.*
To Haswell	2	0	·1	6
To Castle Eden .	1	0	0	9

Dock Office, Hartlepool, 18th Feb. 1841.

FROM J. PROCTER'S, OFFICE, HARTLEPOOL.

1844 Railway notice. Uncorrected proof.
243×152 mm.

Railway Conveyance

OF

GOODS, GRAIN,

FURNITURE, &c.,

At Reduced Rates of Carriage, by the Brandling Junction, Newcastle, and Darlington, Clarence, Stockton and Hartlepool Railways.

Jas. & Isaac Thompson,

RAILWAY CARRIERS,

Respectfully inform the Public that they have made arrangements for the conveyance of Goods, &c., &c. by the above named Railways, to and from the following places.

NEWCASTLE	FERRY HILL
GATESHEAD	COXHOE
SOUTH SHIELDS	SHINCLIFFE
MONKWEARMOUTH	FENCE HOUSES
DURHAM	HOUGHTON-LE-SPRING
HARTLEPOOL	HETTON-LE-HOLE
SEATON	SEAHAM HARBOUR and the
STOCKTON	NEWCASTLE & CARLISLE
DARLINGTON	RAILWAY STATION

Goods forwarded to all parts of the North of England and Scotland

☞ **Orders for Goods forwarded by Post addressed to J. and I. Thompson, Railway Carriers, Brandling Junction Railway Station, Gateshead, will be attended to without the least delay.**

Gateshead, July, 1844

J. PROCTER, PRINTER, HIGH STREET, HARTLEPOOL.

c. 1850 Billhead for ship chandler.
150 × 207 mm.

c. 1850 Billhead for grocer and ship chandler.
205 × 162 mm.

c. 1850 Billhead for ship chandler and sail maker.
80 × 207 mm.

Engraved letterheads changed in character as the nineteenth century advanced. To begin with, little more than the engraving of the shop sign illustrated the formally engraved English copper plate hand. With the advance of the nineteenth century, as can be seen from these Hartlepool billheads, pictures of places of business began to appear against both the English hand and the more decorative engraved letters that often followed the designs of contemporary typefaces.

All three designs on this page were for ship chandler and provision merchants; on the opposite page no doub Mr Martyn the undertaker buried those sailors who wer lucky enough to die ashore; Mr Whaley provided them with clocks and compasses and only Mr Matthew Carte was earthbound with his chimney pots and marbl chimney pieces. Carter's bill to John Procter, the Hartle pool printer, is for some drainage work.

c. 1842 Billhead for draper.
264×206 mm.

1849 Billhead for clock and compass maker.
190×153 mm.

1832 Billhead for chimney top dealer.
170×207 mm.

London & Hartlepool
OLD ESTABLISHED

REGULAR   TRADER.

The fine first Class and fast sailing Schooner,

THE AIR,

Captain Robert Lofthouse,

As arrived in London, and is now laying on at Messrs. W. J. Hall & Co's Wharf, Wool Quay, Thames Street, for Goods and Passengers for Hartlepool and the Neighbourhood;—She will positively clear and sail from London on   the   day of

For Freight or Passage, apply to
Thomas Hunter, Agent, Hartlepool.

J, PROCTER, PRINTER, HARTLEPOOL.

£5.
Reward

On the Morning of Saturday the 18th inst. a number of SAILORS, who by way of intimidation to the Crew of the Ship "John White", did throw a quantity of Stones and Bricks, most of which fell into the Harbour;—any person who shall give such information as may lead to the conviction of any of the Offenders shall receive the above reward from the Hartlepool Dock and Railway Company.

DOCK OFFICE, HARTLEPOOL,
18TH SEPT. 1841.

J. Procter, Printer, Hartlepool.

The North East coast is an unfriendly coast for any sailing vessel. With an onshore wind there are very few harbours which are safe to enter. A modern sailing vessel close-hauled can make her way out to sea in reasonable weather. Little brigs and top-sailed schooners were not weatherly craft. If a strong north-east wind was blowing, most of this coast was a lee shore and parts of it were an absolute death trap – particularly Tees Bay. Here the only hope was for a vessel to try and turn into Hartlepool harbour or failing that for the skipper to beach his craft on the Middleton or New Stranton Sands. The admiralty chart today marks no less than five wrecks within a couple of miles of the entrance to Hartlepool harbour. If the ship missed the Long Scar Rocks, there were the awful West Scar and Salt Scar reefs off Redcar at the south-east end of Tees Bay. South of that there are nearly fifty miles of steep cliffs and off-lying rocks before a vessel could find shelter on the other side of Flamborough Head. In one night during the great storm of 1861, sixty ships were wrecked or beached just between Seaton and the Old Town pier.

Within twenty-four hours of a ship being wrecked, the owners or the underwriters would save what they could and then put the wreck up for auction. Often there was barely time to rescue anything before another storm had completed the destruction of the vessel.

The notice about the auction of the wrecked sloop *Lark* of Woodbridge at Seaton Carew is a link with the previous chapter.

c. 1880 Letterhead for Edward Withy & Co. Ship builder.
Lithographed from a steel engraving.
260 × 208 mm.

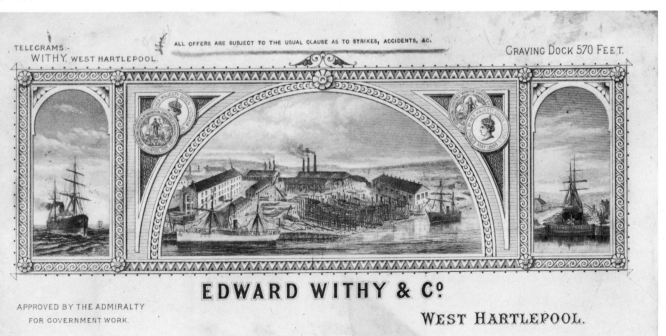

A CHEAP TRIP TO
SUDERLAND.

THE
STEAM BOAT
Middlesbro'

Mr. Jas. Smart, Commander,

Will leave Hartlepool for Sunderland at 8 o'clock
on Sunday Morning next, the 25th inst. Returning
the same day in the Evenning.—Fares there and back
1s. 6d.

Parties visiting Sunderland by the above Boat
may have the pleasure of witnessing the removing of
the Stupendous Lighthouse, (now placed upon the
Pier at Sunderland) a distance of nearly 50 yards.

Hartlepool, July 20th, 1841.

J. Procter, Printer, Hartlepool.

NEWCASTLE RACES
and the celebrated
SKIFF RACE
between
H. Clasper and R. Newell.
on Monday next.

FARE,
THERE
AND
BACK,
2s.

FARE,
THERE
AND
BACK,
2s.

The splendid and powerful steamboat
ROBERT AND ANN,
John Oxley, commander, will leave Hartlepool for Shields
MONDAY, 22nd JUNE,
at six o'clock in the Morning, and will return the same evening.

The well-known prowess of the competing parties, and the heavy sums staked upon the result of this trial of their skill, will, it is expected, induce persous from all parts of the kingdom to be at Newcastle on that day; but should the weather continue as it is, the Tyne will, no doubt, eohibit a scene whibh for gaiety, animation, and bustle, may never again be witnessed. The opportunity thus offered should not be lost by the lovers of pleasure.

Hartlepool, June 18, 1846.

Printed by J. PROCTER, Hartlepool.

WRECKED VESSEL AND STORES.

To be Sold

BY AUCTION,
For the Benefit of the Underwriters,

Messrs. SOTHERAN, AUCTIONEERS,

On *MONDAY*, the 3rd September, 1838,

ON REDCAR AND MARSK SANDS,

ALL THE

WRECK of the HULL of the BRIG

SALEM,

Of Newcastle, Burthen 241 tons Register, A. I.
AS IT WILL THEN LAY IN LOTS.

**Also, all the STORES of the above Vessel, now lying at Mr. Smith's,
Innkeeper, Redcar,**

**Consisting of Lower MASTS, BOWSPRIT, Standing and Running RIGGING,
ANCHORS, KEDGES, CHAIN CABLES, CHAIN HAWSER, TOW LINE
WARPS, TOP-MAST, YARDS, BOOMS and other SPARS, SAILS, BOATS,
WINDLASS, PUMPS, PUMP-GEAR, &c. &c.**

N. B. All the above STORES are in good condition.

The Sale to begin at 10 o'clock in the Morning, and will continue until all are sold.

J. PROCTER, PRINTER, HARTLEPOOL.

SEATON CAREW.

TO BE SOLD BY AUCTION,

On Tuesday, the 27th day of February, 1844,

AT SEATON CAREW, IN THE COUNTY OF DURHAM,

MR. HENRY LAYBOURN, AUCTIONEER,

The WRECK of the Sloop

"LARK"

of Woodbridge, now lying on the Beach near Seaton,

Consisting of Beams, Keelson, Knees, Plank, Deck Deals, and sundry other materials. The Mast, Spars, Sails, Rigging and other Stores are expected to be got this day, in which case they will be sold at the same time.

Sale to commence at one o'clock precisely.

Hartlepool, 26th February, 1844.

J. PROCTER, PRINTER, UNION PLACE, HARTLEPOOL.

1837 Playbill.
375×171 mm.

1848 Playbill. Top part only.
250×170 mm.

c. 1840 Notice advertising a shooting gallery.
142×228 mm.

Great Novelty !!

PURVIS'
SPLENDID THEATRICAL PAVILION,
HARTLEPOOL.

On Tuesday Evening, May 30th, 1837,
Will be presented, the popular domestic Melo-Drama of intense interest, entitled THE

DOG
of Montargis;
Or, the FOREST of BONDY.

Macaire, Lieutenant of the Army, Mr. STANLY.   Colonel Gontram, Mr MATTHEWS.
Captain Aubri, Mr SHELDON   Seneschal, Mr M'INTYRE.
Lieutenant Laundry, Mr ADAMS.   Blaise, Mr ROSS.
Officers, Guards, &c.   Messrs. WALLACE & STEWARD.
Lucille,   Miss ATKINSON.   Dame Gertrude,   Mrs STOKELD.
Annetta, Mrs ROSS.   Florio, the Dumb Boy, Mrs GORDON

**The Part of the Dog Dragon, by Mr Purvis'
Sagacious DOG PEARCY.**

COMIC SONG   ..   ..   MR. MATTHEWS.
HORNPIPE   -   -   -   MASTER GORDON
FAVOURITE SONG, MRS WILLIAMS

To conclude with the laughable Farce of THE

MOCK
DOCTOR;
OR, THE DUMB LADY CURED.

Gregory, a Wood Cutter and Mock Doctor, Mr MATTHEWS.   Leander, Mr SHELDON.
Sir Jasper, Mr ADAMS.   Harry, Mr M'INTYRE.   James, Mr WILLIAMS.
Charlotte, Mrs ROSS.   Dorcas, Mrs STOKELD.
Servant.   Mrs GORDON

DOORS OPEN AT 7 O'CLOCK, AND COMMENCE AT 8.
Boxes & Pit 1s.—Gallery 6d.
MR ADAMS, STAGE-MANAGER.

From the Office of J. PROCTER, High Street, Hartlepool.

By Permission of the Worshipful the Mayor.
VICTORIA THEATRE, HARTLEPOOL
UNDER THE
MANAGEMENT OF Mr. T. MATTHEWS.

First and only time this Season of
The Ocean Child
First and only time also of the COMIC PANTOMIME of
THE HOUSE THAT JACK BUILT,
In which the Celebrated
BILLY PURVIS
Will once more
STEAL THE BUNDLE,
BY DESIRE and under the PATRONAGE of the
CAPTAINS OF THE FLEET
AT PRESENT IN THE HARBOUR,
Who wish once more to witness his Original Comicalities, with which for many years they have been so
delighted, and have justly entitled him the Hero of Northumberland, and
EMPEROR OF CLOWNS!!!

On TUESDAY EVENING, OCTOBER 31st, 1848,
Will be presented the admired Nautical Drama of
THE SEA
Or, The Ocean Child.

Captain Mandeville.....................Mr M'INTYRE—Captain Sturdy ....Mr ROBSON
Snowball...Mr CAMPBELL—Peter Poultice......Mr T. MATTHEWS—Korek......Mr WADFORTH
Harry Helm (a sailor on board the " Windsor Castle," father of the Ocean Child......Mr STEPHENSON
Dennis O'Trot......Mr ALEXANDER—Neptune......Mr THOMPSON—Ocean Child......Miss LAIRD
Mary Helm..Mrs JULIA CAMPBELL

A period of eighteen years is supposed to have elapsed between the first and second acts.

Sir Arthur Hamilton, formerly known as Captain Mandeville ....Mr M'INTYRE
Dennis O'Trot ....Mr ALEXANDER—Doctor Poultice ....Mr T. MATTHEWS

NOTICE.
THE
Shooting
GALLERY
IS NOW OPEN FOR PRACTICE.
In Mr. France's Long Room,
TURF HOTEL, NORTHGATE, HARTLEPOOL.
Entrance Fee,---1d. each Shot.
Doors open from 10 in the Morning till 10 at Night.

J. Procter, Printer, High Street, Hartlepool.

In the nineteenth century, in places like Hartlepool, people worked hard, but they played hard as well. Events like the visit to the Victoria Concert Hall on Monday 14 February 1870 of a music hall show with Townsend and Coulson, the Champion Darkies, the Great Ricardo and his family of Sensational Acrobats, the Brothers Wainratta, the Invisible Wire Walkers and various other acts were enjoyed to a degree present-day television-jaded audiences would find hard to credit.

The Victoria Concert Hall, which was later known as the Theatre Royal, provided entertainment for nearly fifty years until it was pulled down in 1900. Circuses such as Manders' Menagerie usually set up their tents on the outskirts of the town.

In 1837 a much-loved theatrical showman and comedian called Billy Purvis first appeared at Hartlepool. Like most strolling players, he set up his own portable theatre, which in the bill of that year he refers to as his 'Splendid Theatrical Pavilion'. On this occasion Purvis was not taking part in any of the acts, but his 'sagacious dog' Pearcy was. However, that year he ran a season at Hartlepool and presented thirteen separate double feature programmes. Over the years Purvis built up a tremendous following. There was one particular act called 'Stealing the Bundle' which he was made to repeat over and over again. The fact that his audiences knew exactly what was coming only seemed to heighten their ecstatic enjoyment. For a month after Billy Purvis's death in 1853 the playbills for the theatres in which he had performed were all set within a deep mourning border of black. The older people in Hartlepool still remember their grandfathers talking about this immortal character, and his gravestone in the churchyard below St Hilda's church is still kept in immaculate condition.

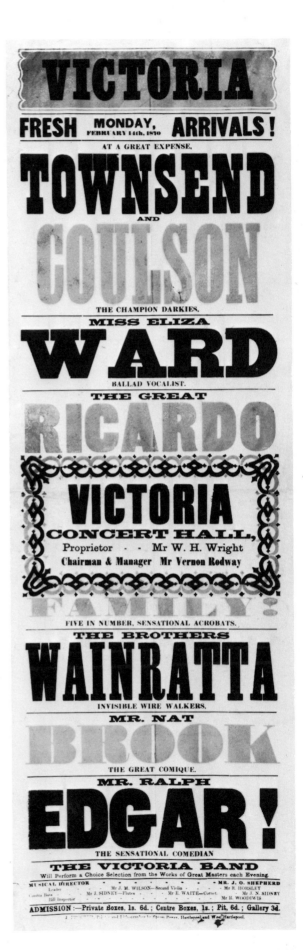

8. Just collecting

As we have seen, printed ephemera provides marvellous back-up material to all kinds of activities, but of course it can be collected in its own right. The most obvious examples of this are postage stamps, cigarette cards, Christmas cards, postcards and matchbox labels. And there are other labels, such as for food stuffs or for wines and spirits, pharmaceutical or even the hardware trade. Any one of these areas could occupy a collector for a life time!

Postage stamp collecting, for instance, is a huge subject – a world of its own, but even here by defining some specialized area a collection could be built up outside the normal run of stamp collecting. Cigarette cards, even though they are no longer printed, are not very expensive in comparison with stamps. They can still be bought from dealers and they come up for sale quite frequently in London and New York salerooms and in country auctions. Again specialization is important, or collections can become most unwieldy.

The collecting of picture postcards was very popular in late Victorian times. Albums were filled with views of holiday places or with drawings of robust humour. Old postcards are probably a more rewarding area for collectors than the slick modern productions. Albums of such cards are always turning up in sales or through the second-hand book trade. The hobby is now called 'deltiology' – a term invented by Randall Rhoades of Ashland, Ohio.

Matchbox label collectors call themselves 'phil-lumenists'. The hobby is older than even stamp collecting and is allied to book-match collecting which is very popular in the USA, and is something that needs little finance. Matchbox labels are often picturesque and some-times objects of folk art.

Earlier in this book we discussed Valentine and Christmas cards. The latter offer a relatively easy field for collection. Each Christmas you select the best of those you have received, or the most original or those with a particular theme. If your friends happen to be designers and artists, their Christmas offerings are often amusing and for sentiment, if for no other reason, are worth hoarding.

Invitation cards, particularly to exhibitions and galleries, over the years can give a revealing picture of the artistic climate of a country or a city at a particular time.

The one thing you must do is to write the date in pencil on the back of every bit of printed ephemera you collect. It is only too easy to forget which year, even which decade a Christmas card or invitation was received. The value of such material to the social historian is considerably enhanced by proper documentation. This may also include putting the sender's full name on the back. You may know who Lonnie or Fuzz was, and that in fact those nicknames hide the identity of someone who one day may be famous. The collector of your material in twenty years time probably will not have the slightest idea who they were.

Postage stamps

There must be thousands, if not millions, of people throughout the world who collect stamps. The hobby was certainly established by 1861, for in that year a catalogue of stamps was issued in Paris. One of the first great dealers was Stanley Gibbons, a Devon man who was born in Paris and was the founder of the firm that still bears his name. Gibbons had been born in 1840, the year Rowland Hill introduced penny postage and the year the Penny Black, the first adhesive stamp, was printed. Today the *Gibbons Simplified Stamp Catalogue* is probably the best guide for the new collector. In addition, there are many books on the subject (see Bibliography).

Stamp collecting can take many forms. It can be for an investment, but for this you have to know what you are doing and catalogues from either Stanley Gibbons or Scotts (in the USA) are essential. More enjoyably stamp collecting can be based on some particular theme – and pictorial themes on postage stamps are legion. Even here it may benefit a new collector to join a stamp collecting society. There may well be one in his locality. There are also innumerable societies dealing with one particular country. These societies are listed in the British Philatelic Association's Handbook and the American title for their handbook. They issue their own magazines and provide an Exchange and Mart operation which can be a great help to the beginner.

The theme system of collecting can range from the relatively unsophisticated collection of stamps with, say pictures of celebrities on them, to the use of stamps, like other printed ephemera in this book, to illustrate a story or a theme.

Stamp collecting, in its purist, classical form, is concerned with the study of stamps as objects. The thematic collector regards the stamps merely as vehicles for carrying illustrations of animals, people, things, places or events Such uses are too obvious to need description. However, the use of stamps to tell a story or illustrate a theme is a different matter. Combined with the use of covers, franked and dated, all kinds of events can be described, such as the siege of Paris during the Franco-Prussian war or the sinking of the *Titanic* or the *Lusitania*, or Orville and Wilbur Wright's first heavier-than-air flight, or less dramatically a theme showing the changes in printing processes used in stamp production.

The study of these printing methods offers an interesting and useful background to stamp collection. The more the collector knows about these different processes the better able he is to judge the quality of the stamps. The Penny Black with the young Queen Victoria's head in classical profile was not only the first stamp to be printed, but also and arguably, the most beautiful stamp ever printed. The stamp was engraved on steel, with an 'engine-turned' background after a drawing which was done from a medal. Line engraving, such as was used for the Penny Black is still in use, and is unbeatable for precision and

1964 First day cover and stamps designed by David Gentleman RDI.
115×184 mm.

1974 & c. 1965 Canadian stamps. French stamp: painting by Marc Chagall.
40×24 mm & 53×42 mm.

sharpness of detail, if used for single or two-colour printings.

Photo-gravure is a photo-mechanical method of intaglio engraving. It is good for rich colouring, poor for sharp detail. Photo-offset lithography is the most widely used method for stamp printing, or any other printing for that matter. It is much crisper than gravure, excellent for line and colour. It is not as effective for half-tone work. In gravure, sunken pits (as opposed to dots) made by the half-tone screen merge into one another, giving a pleasant soft effect. The 150-line screen dots of the offset process are too obtrusive. The scale of the dot is too large for the size of the image on the stamp.

Letterpress printing, that is printing from raised type and blocks, is still used for stamps, though no doubt it will soon be superseded by offset and gravure. Some early stamps were actually printed from type. The first issues from Hawaii were produced in this manner by American missionaries writing to their families back home.

Finally some stamps are embossed. That is the paper is squeezed between a male and female die, thus producing a design in relief. It was first used for the earliest high denomination (one shilling) British stamp, with Queen Victoria's head in relief in white against a coloured background.

In the minds of most collectors of printed ephemera, the visual or historical aspect of postage stamps probably matters more than their philatelic value. Stamps are often more interesting when left *in situ* on their envelopes. The franking can be as picturesque as the stamp itself.

'First Day covers', which commemorate the first day of an issue, are a somewhat artificial method of marketing new stamps. They are prepared specially for collectors, and dealers are the main source of supply. They can be collected to satisfy an interest in some particular theme, such as war or aeronautics. (There is an interesting collection of air freighted covers in the aeronautical section of the Science Museum, London.)

Stamps like any other form of printed ephemera need to be properly documented. There is no need to write a book about each stamp, but captions if succinct, should at least be explanatory and dated.

1850 Engraved letterhead.
190×120 mm.

Postcards

Decorated notepaper with engraved views of the place preceded picture postcards by many years. Such notepaper was certainly in use in the 1830s and possibly earlier. A pretty if naïve example of 'A South View of Worthing taken from the sea' was published in 1832.* The letterhead dated 185- with a street scene of Carnarvon, was almost certainly produced for the benefit of visitors to the Welsh town, who were staying at the Sportsman Inn.

The first picture postcards came into use in the Franco-Prussian war, during the seige of Paris. These postcards only weighed 3 grammes and were transmitted by balloon post. Within twenty years, cards, chromo-lithographed in full and often garish colours, were being produced by the tens of thousands. Soon after the turn of the century over seven billion cards were being sent by post annually. Collecting these cards became a craze. The card publishers issued postcard magazines as an aid to their sales. In 1906 Raphael Tuck, one of the most productive of the postcard publishers, was offering large money prizes 'for the best use of postcards for decorating screens, cupboard lids, overmantels and other objects'.† In 1903 a Glasgow newspaper editor bemoaned the fact that 'In ten years Europe will be buried beneath picture postcards.'‡

The most famous of the comic picture postcard artists was Donald McGill, with his cheerfully immodest post cards of well-developed females and their woefully inadequate consorts, usually captioned with the broadest *double entendres*. Artists who drew for this form of popular art included Charles Dana Gibson in the USA, Tom Browne and Phil May in Great Britain and Alphonse Mucha and Raphael Kirchener on the Continent. Donald McGill's work was mentioned as early as 1905 in *The Picture Postcard Magazine* and the original drawings for these cards were fetching high prices in a London Auction Room in 1974.

The collecting of picture postcards has reached such respectable proportions that one collection is housed in the Metropolitan Museum in New York. This was assembled by J.R. Burdick, who, in 1953 listed as many as twenty postcard collecting clubs in his *American Card Catalogue*.

* Shown in *The Picture Postcard and its Origins* Frank Staff, Lutterworth Press London; Praeger, New York 1966.
† *Pictures in the Post*, Richard Carline. Gordon Fraser, London 1959.
‡ *Picture Postcards,* Marian Klamkin, Rural Life Series, London 1973.

1974 Washing powder packets.
256 × 171 mm.

Labels and packaging

Labels for food and drink and packages for household goods offer an enormous field for the collector of ephemera. The wrapping papers and boxes of the tobacco trade have perhaps the longest history, with the possible exception of the pharmaceutical trade. Both are ideal subjects for an historical collection, providing one can find the early examples. There are fine collections of tobacco labels with the Imperial Tobacco Company at Bristol and at the William R. Perkins Library, Duke University in North Carolina; and pharmaceutical labels at the Wellcome Museum in London.

In some trades, such as tobacco, the continuity of themes is interesting, the blackamoor's head, the Indian smoking a pipe and the sailing ship and dockside scenes occur again and again in tobacco labels and on cigarette boxes. The Royal Coat of Arms and the American Eagle are often repeated on pin packets and other hardware

labels. Tea bags inspired endlessly repeated versions of Chinamen and pagodas.

Grocer's labels and printed bags have a long tradition. There are some in the British Museum dating back to the mid-eighteenth century. Food still inspires label and box designs that are gay and bright, and sometimes very decorative.

Sociologically the most revealing designs are reserved for washing detergents, with their claims of 'Whiter than white', 'Bumper size' and '2p off'. A study of such packaging practices might include the work of quack pill merchants and cheapjack clothiers. In fact a fascinating collection could be built up on this theme, either confining it to contemporary packaging, or as a comparative study of, say, early nineteenth century hucksters and modern supermarket practice.

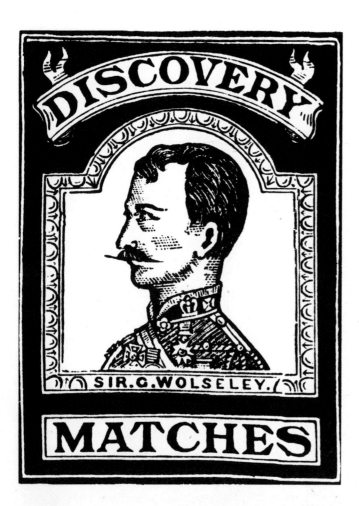

Matchbox labels

Some of the prettiest labels come from Japan. The work of Utamaro and Hiroshige has frequently appeared on matchboxes. Reproductions of Hiroshige's fifty-five drawings of the Tokaido Road first appeared on the boxes before 1900 and have been repeated many times. Relatively recently, twelve pictures of the Kabuki Theatre have been printed on matchbox labels. Works of art have been reproduced on labels in various countries including China and Mexico.

In spite of these handsome reproductions, the more naïve designs are perhaps more interesting. The first pictorial label appeared in Britain in 1830, it was an unintentionally comic design of a Highlander and a Sassenach smoking. It also had two serpents blowing out a flame and a Royal Coat of Arms. The whole thing was printed on a bilious green background. The first friction match had only been invented some five years earlier, by a Stockton-on-Tees chemist called John Walker.

Although book matches have largely replaced boxed matches in the USA, early American match labels crop up at auctions. Nearly forty years ago an auction of matchbox labels took place at Harrisburg in Pennsylvania. A rare label picturing a horse and trap and with the words 'Sulphur Matches manufactured by V. R. Powell in Troy N.Y.' was withdrawn from sale at $100. A dealer afterwards priced this label at $350.

A law in the USA prohibiting the transportation of matches by railroad resulted in a great number of small match factories being established right across the continent. From the time of the Civil War up to 1885 there was a stamp duty on the sale of matches. Each factory was allowed to design its own stamp providing it had on it the words 'U.S. Internal Revenue' printed on it. These stamps were usually intaglio engraved and often carried portraits of the manufacturers. They provide a separate and interesting field for the collector.

The hobby of collecting matchbox labels has had some royal support, from Queen Wilhelmina of Holland, King Alfonso of Spain, King Farouk of Egypt and more than some from the King of Siam, the one who had eighty-two wives, over seventy children and who expired at the age of fifty-seven in 1910, not surprisingly worn out. Still, he had time to assemble a large collection of matchbox labels. One famous collector, who was the owner of the Oxenham Arms in South Zeal, Devon covered the entire wall of one bedroom with 11,000 matchbox labels.

Matchbox label collecting, like stamp collecting, can be divided up in many ways, such as by countries. The main match manufacturing countries are Sweden, Austria, Great Britain, Czechoslovakia, Norway, Finland, Belgium, Holland, Spain, Egypt, Japan, China and India. For instance, Sweden has produced over 40,000 different matchbox label designs since the industry was started there by Johann Edward Lundstrom in 1844. The most famous series of Swedish labels was a set of sixty different nursery rhymes.

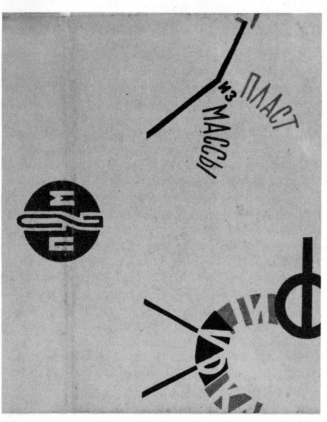

The other and obvious way of breaking down this hobby to manageable proportions is by concentrating on one subject. Various labels have been issued commemorating famous people, such as sportsmen (there is an 1875 label design of Captain Webb swimming the English Channel, and another in 1908 of Dorando the Italian marathon runner) and national heroes such as Captain Cook or Garibaldi. There have been plenty of designs including royal personages on matchbox labels. The Netherlands have frequently used Queen Wilhelmina on their matchboxes but Austria seems to have produced more matchbox labels than anyone else with other country's royalty portrayed on them. King Edward VII and Queen Alexandra did not escape their net, nor did the German Kaiser, King Gustav of Sweden nor King Carol of Rumania.

Book matches come under a different category, but are none the less collectable. The United States was the first country to replace matchboxes with book matches and the collection of these has become very popular in the USA. As a vehicle for publicity, the book matches have been used by restaurants, bars, hotels, passenger ships, airlines and railways. The covers should not be cut. Just pull out the staples and let the matches drop out. Clean them and press them flat.

Cigarette cards

I started collecting cigarette cards when I was a small boy in the early twenties. The first set I completed was a series issued by W.D. & H.O. Wills called Do You Know? This was one of many series of cards that had an educational bias. Among the gratuitous information offered in the fifty Do You Know? cards was the meaning of the Plimsoll line, how bees sting, the mysteries of the Sargasso Sea and the meaning of hallmarks on silver. By assiduous and selective collecting and due study of the legends on the back of the cards it was possible to acquire a considerable of superficial knowledge of practically every subject under the sun.

The earlier cards usually had no texts on the back but when I started collecting I was given an album of cards issued before 1912; many of these had blank backs. This I learned later was probably because they were issued abroad in a country where literacy was not prevalent. There was a set of Drum Horses and another of British Regiments and they had indeed no indication of the tobacco manufacturer who had issued them.

The earliest cards quite often were issued with just the manufacturer's name and an ornamental design on the back, such as a set of Dancing Girls of all Nations. These were actually issued by W.D. & H.O. Wills and there was a tobacco leaf design surrounding their name. Another very early set without descriptive text on the back was Locomotives issued by Wills in 1901. Locomotives crop up over the years. Wills issued three other sets on the subject, one of which I collected in 1924.

Cigarette cards began as stiffeners in the paper packets that usually contained five cigarettes although if they were offered in a larger quantity they still had this very flimsy packing in the early days.

The first date which has definitely been established for a cigarette card, an American one, which had the picture of the Marquis of Lorne on it, was 1879 and went with cigarettes of the same brand name. The Marquis of Lorne was the son of the Duke of Argyll and was, at that time, Governor General of Canada. Wills was one of the first British Tobacco Companies to issue sets of cigarette cards.

In the USA several hundred sets were issued before 1900 and a very large proportion of these were of pretty girls, actresses or baseball heroes and other sporting personalities, but the American scene was a common theme in the USA as indeed was the British Empire with the British cigarette manufacturers. A tobacco war between the American and British firms in which cigarette cards played an important part came to an end in 1902 with the establishment of the British American Tobacco Company. This was formed to handle the cigarette trade outside Great Britain; and the Imperial Tobacco Company (which was a combination of Wills, Players, Lambert & Butler and various other firms) held almost a monopoly for the United Kingdom and a wide area of British-held territories. However, although the wording 'Imperial Tobacco Co. of Great Britain and Ireland Ltd' was usually added to the card, it did not stop the separate firms within this group continuing to issue many different sets of cards under their original names of Wills, Players, Ogdens etc.

Sets of cards usually comprise fifty or twenty-five but in the very large cards which were packed with packets of fifty or 100, sometimes the sets consisted only of ten or twelve. There was one curious set of Characters from R. L. Stevenson's *Treasure Island* issued by B. Morris & Co. London, with their Lawn Virginia Cigarettes round about 1925, which had only thirteen cards. The cards in packets of ten cigarettes measured approximately $2\frac{5}{8} \times 1\frac{3}{8}$ in. (68×36 mm.) Larger cards which came with twenty

CARP

CORKWING WRASSE

cigarettes were approximately $3\frac{1}{8} \times 2\frac{1}{2}$ in. (80×62 mm), whereas with the fifties and hundreds they could be even larger. Such cards were issued among others by John Player & Sons in their Characters from Dickens, Natural History etc.

As for the practicalities of collecting cigarette cards, it might seem a strange hobby today. To all intents and purposes, tobacco manufacturers stopped issuing cigarette cards at the beginning of the Second World war. Tea manufacturers such as Brooke Bond have, however, continued the tradition.

The cigarette cards which fetch really high values are those issued between 1880 and 1900 but from 1902 and the formation of the Imperial Tobacco Company the cards were put out in larger numbers, and some sets latterly even had a print run of over 400 million so there is obviously no rarity value here. However, they still have the regard of collectors as covetable things and can be bought even today quite inexpensively from stamp dealers or junk shops, but particularly from the London Cigarette Card Co. Ltd. of Chiswick, W4, who have become known as the Stanley Gibbons of the cigarette card world in their nearly fifty years of trading.

There is nothing comparable to the London Cigarette Card Company in the United States, where cigarette cards largely ceased to be issued after 1905.

When collecting early cards — and some sets such as Macdonald's Cricketers and Taddy's Clowns may cost several hundred pounds if in excellent condition — watch out for just this one factor: condition. It is, of course, a key point in any collecting be it books, stamps or cigarette cards, and these latter, passing through the grubby hands of little boys, are often far from clean. It is cheaper to buy at a higher price from a specialist firm, such as the one I have quoted, and obtain a set in fine condition, which will not only continue to give you pleasure, but will also be an investment, than to pay less for a grubby set which will always be an eyesore and of no investment value.

Reynolds

The Fortune Teller
B.D.V. CIGARETTES

1935 Sizes of cigarette and trade cards. Fresh-water fishes (series of 25) issued by John Player & Sons.
Large size 62×79 mm.
Sea fishes (series of 50) issued by John Player & sons.
36×68 mm.

1974 The Sea — our other world (series of 50) issued by Brooke Bond Oxo Ltd.
37×68 mm.

c. 1925 BDV Silks: Old Masters: set 6 (series of 50) issued by Godfrey Phillips. These 'cards' were beautifully printed on unbacked silk. *John W. Townsend Collection*.
67×42 mm.

The typography of printed ephemera

Any pre-1800 printed ephemera worth looking at was almost certainly engraved on copper or steel. The engravers of letterheads and trade cards were at their peak in the eighteenth century when they could indulge in all the vagaries of baroque and rococo decoration. The work of the letterpress printer, apart from crude woodcuts, showed little sense of design. In fact ephemeral printing remained bookish in format from the time the roman letter was adopted in England in the early fifteen hundreds, until Robert Thorne, of the Fann Street Typefoundry in London, produced his Fat Face, the first real display typeface, in 1803.

From then on, and for the next three quarters of a century in both England and the United States, the jobbing printer or his compositor made artless but often brilliant use of an ever-increasing range of display letters. Thorne was the great innovator and produced, long before anyone else, Fat Faces and fat Egyptians which were, to quote Talbot Baines Reed, 'Unique for their boldness and deformity'.

Not every printer and typefounder approved of Robert Thorne's innovations, or indeed of the success of William Thorowgood, his successor at Fann Street. Vincent Figgins, a rival English display typefounder, said in 1823 in a specimen sheet of his 'Two-line Great Primer Antique': 'The increased fatness in job letters is an improvement but is it not in many instances carried to an extreme?' And in 1828, Dr Edmund Fry, a letter founder, who had a considerable custom with the Americas, said that after forty-six years he had decided to dispose of his foundry. After starting with improved versions of Baskerville's typefaces, he had found that there was more favour given to the Caslon style of letter, so he had set about copying all Caslon's types. He had no sooner completed these copies of the productions of the Chiswell Street foundry, when, as he goes on to say: '. . . a rude and pernicious and most unclassical innovating system was commenced, which in a short time was followed by the most injurious and desolating ravages on the property of every Letter Founder and Printer in the Kingdom, by the introduction of Fancy letters, of various anomalous forms, with names as appropriate. Disgraceful is a profession once held so sacred as to have its operations confined to sacred buildings of the highest class . . .'

Thorne and Thorowgood did not share Dr Fry's regret, nor on the other side of the Atlantic did the Wells family at the Cincinnati Type Foundry. The productions of the jobbing printer in both the USA and in Britain between 1810 and 1880 showed a splendid appreciation of this new typographic material, whether for starkly printed notices or for highly complicated playbills, for railway tickets or tobacco labels. This vitality, the product of somewhat naïve craftsmen, was not to be recaptured again in jobbing printing until the middle of the twentieth century. In the 1880s, with a great increase of mechanization in printing, two movements sprang up, both largely fostered by *The Printers' International Specimen Exchange* published by

Messrs Field and Tuer at the Leadenhall Press in London.

The two movements were called 'Artistic Printing' and 'Antique Printing'. In the former, the compositor attempted the task of producing a formula for jobbing printing that owed nothing either to book-work or to the vigorous displays of the earlier years of the century. This formula consisted of an asymmetrical arrangement of panels of colour, patterns of printers' ornaments and brass rules bent and twisted in all kinds of unlikely ways.

'Antique Printing' was the particular pride of the Leadenhall Press's printer Andrew Tuer, who styled himself 'Olde style or antique printer'. For this sort of work he used seventeenth-century chapbook cuts or pastiche seventeenth-century cuts by Joseph Crawhall, early nineteenth-century borders and late nineteenth-century typefaces, which were battered about to give them a feeling of antiquity. Some of his work was not without charm.

These movements soon exhausted themselves and gave way to the spaciousness of Art Nouveau, with its oriental overtones, and later to the restrained good manners of the revival of Renaissance printing. It was not until the New Movement in Typography got under way in the 1920s, when through the work and experiment of such men as Moholy-Nagy and Herbert Bayer at the Bauhaus and the writings of Jan Tschichold, a new light was shed on the problems of ephemeral printing.

Yet the impact of this new thinking was slow to have much effect on the appearance of ephemera. Some new sans serif typefaces were cut. Those in Germany were based on the antics of the compass and set-square; those in England on classical Renaissance letterforms. It was not until mid-twentieth-century printers and typographers rediscovered (and also re-drew) the nineteenth-century grotesque letter that they had a type form that really matched their needs. For, like architects, they had turned their backs on Renaissance culture and also on traditional typography.

Ephemeral printing has a longer history than book printing and by its unselfconsciousness often provides a truer picture of the time. The scope of the subject is endless, for a lot of ephemera has been printed since Caxton set up his press in the precincts of Westminster Abbey, or even since 1732, when Benjamin Franklin printed and published his *Poor Richard's Almanack* in Philadelphia.

Much of this book is taken up with nineteenth-century ephemera, for that was when the fun began and it became really interesting. The change in style of printed ephemera at the beginning of the nineteenth century came about a little more slowly in the USA, but once the American typefounders really got into production with these new display types, they soon caught up their English rivals and by the last quarter of the century had surpassed them in the variety of their display letters and had made considerable inroads into their markets.

Most of the illustrations in this book that date from

London Orphan Asylum.   1821 Thorowgood's Great Primer Black

Fellow Weavers !   1801 Figgins' French Canon No 1 Italic

Set on Fire,   1803 Thorne's 2-line Great Primer Fat Face

EXCURSION   1803 Thorne's French Canon Fat Face

Saturday, Aug. 4.   1821 Thorowgood's 2-line Great Primer Italic Fat Face

EPSOM RACES   1843 Wilson's 5-line Pica Elongated

ALBION   1830 Miller & Richards 5-line Pica Antique (Egyptian)

COUNTRY   1856 French Canon Condensed Egyptian

AUCTION SALE!   1890 American (Vermont) 6-line Pica French Antique (Miller & Richards c. 1865)

CHESTER   1821 Caslon's 2-line Great Primer Italian

VOYAGE MUSICAL   1849 American (N.Y.) 2-line Pica S ns Serif (Stephenson Blake 1838)

HENRY

1905 12-line Pica Wood Letter Sans Serif

150

TO BE SOLD   1808 Fry and Steel's 2-line English Ornamented No 2

W. HOLLOWAY   1817 Figgins 2-line Brevier Shaded

STURMINSTER   1866 2-line Pica Shadow Egyptian

STRONG ALE   Modern revival 2-line English Sans Serif Shaded

CHEAPTRIP   1872 2-line Great Primer Tuscan

KING'S WAGER   1838 Stephenson Blake's 10-line Pica Sans Surryphs Ornamented

NOTICE!   1849 Stephenson Blake's 4-line Pica Ornamented Tuscan

UNION   1842 2-line English Ornamented Tuscan

BY CALEB LEWIS,   1854 Caslon's 2-line Ornamented Tuscan No 4

STEAM NAVICATION   c. 1845 2-line Pica Rustic

EXCURSION   TRAIN   c. 1856 Miller & Richards 2-line Nonpareil Ornamented Tuscan

J. POLITO   c. 1845 German French Canon Ornamented Tuscan

BLENHEIM,   1844 Caslon's 4-line Pica Rounded Ornamented

LIVERPOOL   1842 Caslon's English 2-line Ornamented No 2

1972 Exhibition and Concert bill, printed and designed by Love, Grady and Price of Coventry. 747 × 400 mm.

COVENTRY CATHEDRAL
SATURDAY FEBRUARY 26TH 1972 AT 2.30 PM

SALUTE TO THE 1870s

A look at yesterday, the better to understand today, the better to create tomorrow.

INTERNATIONAL PROGRAMME OF CULTURAL STUDIES
EXHIBITION

The Exhibition will take place in St. Michael's Hall and the Chapter House and is open for all to see from the 26th of February until the 1st of March. Exhibits are by courtesy of the Herbert Art Gallery and Museums; the City Libraries; the City Record Office; the Shakespeare Birthplace Trust; and the Coventry & Warwickshire Collection.

MUSIC CONCERT

at 2.30 p.m. an Organ recital of three chorales by Cesar Franck will be given in the Nave by Professor William Eifrig of Valparaiso University, Indiana, U.S.A. *at 3.30 p.m.* Choral Evensong will be sung by the Coventry Cathedral Choir in the Nave again.

TEA & LECTURE

at 4.30 p.m. Tea will be provided in the Cathedral Refectory. *at 5.00 p.m.* A Public Lecture will be delivered in the Chapter House entitled THE FUTURE THROUGH THE PAST by Maurice Edelman Esq. M.P.

 # PROSE & POETRY

at 8.00 p.m. Readings, Drama and Music CARRY ON VICTORIANS presented by Pauline & Robert Prior-Pitt, and Deborah Templin

Inclusive Ticket Costs 40p
available from the Coventry Cathedral Bookshop
Further Information is available from Van C. Kussrow, Coventry Cathedral, Coventry CV1 5ES.

Designed by Love Grady and Price of Coventry

1971 Exhibition bill published by the National Portrait Gallery.
Designed by Dorothea Smallridge for HMSO and printed by the
Curwen Press.
300×210 mm.

THE
NATIONAL PORTRAIT GALLERY

PRESENTS AN EXHIBITION OF

VICTORIAN
MUSIC COVERS

FEATURING

Miss Marie Lloyd
in
"Oh! Mr. Porter"

Mr. Slade Murray
in
**"Don't leave your mother
when her hair turns grey"**

Miss Nellie Farren
in
**"I'm a Jolly Little
Chap All Round"**

Mr. George Leybourne in
**"Champagne Charlie
is my name"**

AND MANY OTHER FAMILY FAVOURITES
SCENIC EFFECTS By Miss Caroline Brown

ON FRIDAY, DECEMBER 17th, 1971
to SUNDAY, JANUARY 30th, 1972
ADMISSION IS FREE

Hours of Admittance
Monday to Friday .. ten o'clock to five o'clock
Saturday .... ten o'clock to six o'clock
Sunday .... two o'clock to six o'clock

Most of the exhibits are very generously lent from the collection of
MR. JOHN HALL & Mr. DAVID MACWILLIAMS

before 1900 are the products of unsophisticated printers such as Procter in Hartlepool and Loder in Woodbridge. The mid-twentieth-century work that is shown here such as the bills for Coventry and the National Portrait Gallery, are from the hands of typographers who are anything but unsophisticated.

Now, to come to the typefaces. Ephemeral printing reflects the times in which it is printed. The constant and repeating factors are the typefaces in which it is set. Using ephemera, one can trace the development of display typography from the beginning of the nineteenth century up to present times.

The nineteenth century display letters depend on three basic forms: the Sans Serif, the Fat Face and the Egyptian. In chronological order, the Fat Face appeared first, beginning as a semi-fat version of an engraved style of letter, the so-called Modern face, associated particularly with the work of the great Italian printer and type cutter, G. B. Bodoni. This semi-fat form was extended in the full blooded Fat Face with its hair-line serifs and hair-line upstrokes.

The next and probably the most interesting display typeface is the Egyptian. This slab-serifed typeface is based on the sort of letter that was used for shop front fascia boards. It is just as effective in massive ten-line capitals on 'For Sale' posters and playbills as it is in minute Brevier or Minion sizes for tollgate tickets or other small scraps of throw-away printing. Egyptian types were first shown in 1815 in the type book of the Smithfield typefoundry of Vincent Figgins.

The third basic typeform is the Sans Serif which made an unobtrusive appearance in the Caslon Foundry's type-book in 1816. In 1832 Figgins showed a heavier letter. This was followed by variations of condensed sans serifs from a variety of sources, but it was not until the 1850s that satisfactory sans serifs appeared from typefounders on both sides of the Atlantic.

On these three basic forms innumerable type designs were produced, some heavy, some light, some in three-dimensional form and many decorated. The Egyptian went through many metamorphoses, including having its serifs bifurcated to produce a typeface called a Tuscan, which in its turn was decorated and three-dimensionalized, to produce some delightful typographic confections. A bastard variation on the Egyptian was the Italian with the weight transposed from the vertical to the horizontal.

Towards the end of the century, under Art Noveau influence further variations of the basic forms, mostly light in weight, were produced. Some of these were very broken-backed objects, others had a wayward charm.

Typefaces can be a help towards checking the dates of ephemeral printing. At least, one can say that because such and such a typeface was used, the particular piece of paper, be it poster or tollgate ticket, could not have been printed before a certain date, because one or other of the typefaces from which it was printed was not cast before that date.

The checking of typefaces, particularly nineteenth-century display faces, is not an easy task. There is no reference book that neatly tabulates them all.*

It is a matter of going back to source books – to the type specimen books of the various English, American and Continental typefounders. Some at least of these can be found in libraries such as the British Museum Library, the Bibliothèque Nationale in Paris, or the New York Public Library. More can be found in specialist libraries such as St Bride's Printing Library in London or at Columbia University Library in New York, where the American Typefounders Collection is lodged.

Methods of cleaning, collating and filing

Printed ephemera may often need cleaning. When he found John Procter's old spike files, Robert Wood was faced with a cleansing operation that would have made the cleaning of the Augean stables seem like a half-holiday. These five-foot-high files had been stored in a shed under a roof that had half the tiles missing. Not only were these files coated with soot, so that they looked like black Christmas trees, but they were also topped with guano, the droppings of generations of seagulls. These spike files with their accumulations of filth each weighed about 120 lbs (55 kilos). Robert Wood later wrote: 'The only solution was to make use of every fine day to get one out into the garden and slowly strip off each piece of paper and either put it into one box for retention or another for destruction. Those preserved had to be cleaned and I can still see the look of horror on the face of one of the ladies in charge of the Enthoven Collection in the Victoria and Albert Museum laying down one of their posters on a silk screen stiffener, when I said that I got the dirt off my theatre posters by putting them under the tap, then hung them on a clothes line to dry and finished the job by ironing them! Now fifteen years later, I am finished with spike files but still busy sorting out the fragments I retained and cleaning them and taking an occasional look in the guard books. It is a full-time occupation.'

About cleaning, Mr Wood goes on to say: 'I soon discovered that no matter how filthy a sheet of paper was, providing it was not touched by human hand or moistened, it was possible to lift off every particle of dirt and leave a perfectly clean surface below with a wallpaper cleaner on sale known as Walldeco, although for some reason it is now rather difficult to obtain.'

Our procedure for cleaning old pieces of paper is first to dust the front and back with a soft fine brush to get rid of any loose dirt or dust. Then we use either new bread kneaded up into a soft ball, or very soft india rubber from an artists' colourman. When the paper is stained it may be

---

* The only exceptions to this are Nicolette Gray's *Nineteenth Century Ornamented Types and Title-pages*, Faber, London 1938 and Rob Roy Kelly's *American Wood Type 1828–1900*, Van Nostrand, Reinhold, New York 1969.

necessary to wash it. This is of course impossible with coated papers or cards such as cigarette cards, which have a china clay coating to receive the half-tone printing.

Foxing (brown spotted stains caused by damp), may be removed by brushing on a weak solution of chloramine T, in the proportion of ten of water to one of chloramine T, then washing with clean water and drying between sheets of absorbent paper. Some stains can be removed by submerging the paper in hot water that has a little alum in it. Others will yield to soft brushing with pure Castille soap and warm water.

There is a more elaborate method of cleaning and bleaching paper. This is to put the piece of ephemera into a quart of warm water in which an ounce of permanganate of potash has been dissolved. The piece of paper is left in the permanganate solution until — alarmingly — it turns dark brown. This may take an hour or even more. The paper is then taken from the solution and put under running water until all the brown is washed out of it. The paper is then placed in a dish of sulphurous (not sulphuric) acid, diluted to the proportion of one ounce of sulphurous acid to one pint of water. The paper will turn white and the stains should disappear (if they have not, repeat the process more slowly). The paper is next washed in running water for at least an hour, then blotted and hung up over a line to dry. Finally the paper will need re-sizing. This treatment is not suitable for coloured paper.

For sizing the paper, dissolve an ounce of pure gelatine in a quart of water, which when slowly warmed to a temperature of 120°F (50°C) should make a clear solution. Pour the solution into a clean metal baking dish and place over a hot plate to keep the temperature constant. Submerge the piece of ephemera and take out immediately. Place between sheets of blotting paper, press dry, then lay flat on clean paper.

Brown stains will be removed by hot size, so the complicated washing and bleaching process described above may not be necessary. It is important to rub out any dirt and pencil marks, otherwise the size will fix them.

To test the purity of gelatine, soak it in cold water, then pour a little boiling water on to it. If it is not pure, it will stink to high heaven and have a glue-like consistency. If pure, it will have no smell and will form a thick, clear straw-coloured solution.*

Greasy marks can be removed with ether. It should be flooded over the grease spot, a piece of blotting paper should be put on top and a hot iron applied to it.

For coated papers, cleaning is a very different problem. Grubby cigarette cards are probably beyond redemption. The best one can do is to use a very clean, soft rubber.

Crease marks can be taken out of paper by the use of a hot iron.

Methods of collating, mounting and filing will be governed by the material. Stamps of course are always mounted with special adhesive stamp hinges. Incidentally, stamps should always be handled with tweezers. The same hinges can be used for mounting other small pieces of ephemera such as matchbox labels. These should be soaked off the box and dried on a rough towel or blotting paper. Stamp covers (envelopes) can be mounted using special transparent corner pockets. These could also be used for book matches, trade cards, etc. There are also special albums with acetate pockets for covers. Cigarette cards are no problem, for slip-in albums can be bought for this purpose.

Mounting larger pieces of printed ephemera is a more difficult proposition. If the piece of paper is potentially valuable e.g. a fifteenth-century Indulgence, a sixteenth-century Proclamation, a seventeenth-century Trade card, an eighteenth-century type specimen or a nineteenth-century Playbill, then the best thing is not to mount it, but to keep in clean paper folders, or in large acetate pockets.

Small pieces of printed ephemera are much easier to handle if mounted, but large or small, *never* trim them, however tattered they may be. Also never use Scotch tape for mending them. For repairing tears and for pasting down such pieces, use bookbinder's paste. This makes unmounting easier, as the piece of paper can be soaked off in water. For coated papers use rubber cement or Cow gum. For unmounting, the individual piece of paper can be freed from its mount by flooding with rubber cement thinner or lighter fuel respectively. When using these solvents, take care to keep them away from the printing ink, or they will dissolve that as well. If the ink does get damped with these solvents, be very careful not to touch the surface until the fluid has evaporated, or the ink will smear badly.

Filing depends on classification. This may be a simple enough matter for stamps or matchbox labels, but for a subject like the theatre, there is the problem of size, with large playbills and posters, small handbills and programmes and very small tickets. Playbills are best kept in portfolios or Solander cases, which are boxes made in the form of books. For smaller unmounted objects, either box files (or even shoe boxes) will do. When small pieces of ephemera are mounted, I think they are most accessible if kept in drawer files, so that they stand up vertically and can be leafed through with much less trouble than if they were stored flat.

Printed ephemera can be divided by subjects and the subjects can be sub-divided alphabetically. In the case of a thematic collection some other system can be evolved. An almost impossible problem is card indexing, because of the proportions such a collection quickly reaches. The best I can do is to label and group the files and document the individual pieces (an additional reason for mounting). Very large posters I keep in a plan chest, with labelled drawers, but this is not ideal because of the difficulty of searching through a pile of fifty or so items in one drawer.

---

* See *Bookbinding* by Douglas Cockerell, Pitman, London 1925.

Collections of printed ephemera

John Johnson Collection, Bodleian Library, University of Oxford.

John Johnson's 'Sanctuary of Printing' transferred from the Oxford University Press, contains, as he said: '. . . everything which would normally go into the waste paper basket'. Dr Johnson started his collection in 1925, when he became Printer to the University. He bought several collections made by Oxford men and methodically began to put in order these squirrel-like hoardings. Then, through the years, to this basis he added an enormous collection of printed ephemera, including collections of watch papers, Valentines, cigarette cards, banknotes, postage stamps, watermarks. Amongst subjects covered are religion, elections, education, army and navy, trade and finance, agriculture, food and drink, dress, cosmetics, transport, sports, games and , pastimes, entertainment, official notices, indulgences and death.

British Museum Library, London.

Collections of printed ephemera in the British Museum are mostly listed in the catalogue under 'Collections'. The subjects include: almanacs, ballads, broadsides, songs, pamphlets. There are Jacobite leaflets, playbills, etc. for David Garrick and his part in the Shakespeare Jubilee of 1769, leaflets and broadsides about criminal trials, lotteries, catalogues and theatre programmes.

The Joseph Ames Collection has several thousand title-pages and pages of alphabets.

The Bagford Collection includes tobacco wrappers.

The Banks Collection includes prospectuses.

The Fillenham Collection has Christmas cards, 'remarkable characters', 'Fireworks in the Green Park' and posters for menageries.

London Museum, Kensington Palace, London. Jonathan King (Victorian stationer) collection of Valentines.

Newcastle-upon-Tyne Public Library. Collection of Bewick's works ; also volumes of printed ephemera (mostly playbills and election squibs) relating to Tyneside. And at the University Library, some of John Procter's guard books. (Procter was the Hartlepool printer [see pp 113–141].)

Soulby Collection at the **Museum of Rural Life, Reading, Berkshire.**

Soulby Collection at the **Public Library, Barrow-in-Furness,** Lancashire.

American Antiquarian Society. Worcester, Mass.

Historical Society of Pennsylvania. Philadelphia, Pen.

University of Michigan. Ann Arbor, Mich.

New York Public Library, New York. This library has a magnificent collection of material ranging from Benjamin Franklin's *Poor Richard's Almanack* to late nineteenth-century political, travel and theatrical bills.

Bella C. Landauer Collection, **New York Historical Society,** New York.

This collection contains, apart from bookplates and trade cards, fans printed with advertising matter, menus, Valentines, invitations and announcements of social events, lottery tickets, railroad passes, tobacco, beer and other labels, posters and various other kinds of ephemera which give a vivid picture of the professional and business history of America.

William R. Perkins Library (Rare Books), Duke University, Durham, North Carolina.

A collection of over 2,000 items connected with advertising, chiefly of material from the United States, mainly between 1870 and 1970. Also a large but uncatalogued collection to do with tobacco, including cigar wrappers and cigarette packets.

Note: It is worth checking with your local public library and nearest record office or city archives as to whether they have any typographic collections or any printed ephemera.

Typography and typebooks

St Brides Printing Library, London
British Museum Library, London
National Library of Scotland, Edinburgh
Bibliothèque Nationale, Paris
Columbia University Library, New York. American Typefounders Collection
Houghton Library, Harvard Mass
Newberry Library, Chicago

General Collections with some printed ephemera: Transport

Science Museum, London.
Shipping and coastal craft.
Hudson Collection of Railway tickets (60,000) dating from 1870.
Penn-Gaskell Collection of aeronautical ephemera, including stamps and posters.

British Railways Museum, York.
This museum (due to open 1976) contains a wide collection of railway ephemera including posters, documents and tickets.

Syon Park, Brentford, London.
London Transport Collection with over fifty years of historic transport posters, tickets etc.

Museum of Transport, Glasgow.

Great Western Railway Museum, Swindon.

National Maritime Museum, Greenwich, London.
Naval history, miscellaneous ephemera including early recruiting posters.

Smithsonian Institution, Washington D.C.
This great museum has a collection of ephemera covering many facets of transport.

Bath Marine Museum, Bath, Maine.
This museum is becoming a great source of material dealing with maritime history of the Maine coast.

Mystic Seaport, Conn.
One of the great maritime museums of the world, Mystic Seaport has a fine library with much ephemeral material about the New England coast and its sea-faring history.

Peabody Museum, Salem, Mass.
The exhibits are grouped under maritime history, natural history and ethnology.

Penobscot Marine Museum, Searsport, Maine.
An extensive collection of prints and other nautical memorabilia.

Miscellaneous

Victoria and Albert Museum, London.
The Enthoven Collection of the Theatre, with over 200,000 playbills.

Science Museum, London.
Match collection of **Bryant and May**, Bethnal Green, London. Largest collection of matchbox labels in the world.

Circus World Museum, Barbaroo, Wisconsin. Owned by the State Historical Society of Wisconsin.

Postage stamp collections

British Museum, London. A number of very fine collections are housed here including one showing practically every stamp issued between 1840 and 1890.

National Postal Museum. King Edward Building G.P.O. London E.C.1.
Traces story of the postage stamp from its beginning.

Science Museum, London. Penn-Gaskell collection of aeronautical covers.

Imperial War Museum, London. Stamps from the First World War.

Philatelic Bureau, Edinburgh. Organized by the Post Office for the sale of stamps.

Bibliography

Printing 1770–1970, Michael Twyman, Eyre and Spottis-woode, London 1970.
As well as being a history, this contains a large selection of ephemera.

John Soulby, Printer, Ulverston, Museum of English Rural Life, University of Reading 1966.
A study of the work of a provincial printer, between 1796 and 1827.

Printed Ephemera: the changing use of type and letter-forms in English and American Printing, John Lewis, Cowell/Faber & Faber, London; Dover, New York 1962.

Victorian Delights, Robert Wood, Evans Brothers, London; Dover, New York 1967.
The pick of a nineteenth-century printer's jobbing work.

History at Source Series
Children 1773–1890, Robert Wood, Evans Brothers, London; International Publications Service, New York 1968.
Law and Order 1725–1886, Robert Wood, Evans Brothers, London 1970.
other books in the same series all using printed ephemera:
   Entertainment Robert Wood.
   Roads before the Railways J. M. Thomas.
   Factory Life Peter Shellard.

Label Design: the evolution, design and function of labels from the earliest times to the present day, Claude Humbert, Thames & Hudson, London 1972.
This is an historical and comparative study with 1,000 illustrations.

Packaging and Print, Alec Davis, Faber & Faber, London 1967.
Traces the development of containers and label design.

Art for Commerce, illustration and designs in stock at E.S. & A. Robinson, Printers, Bristol in the 1880s. Introduction by Michael Turner and David Vaisey. The Scholar Press, London 1973. (Stock blocks, ornaments etc.).

The Public Notice: an illustrative history, Maurice Rickards, David & Charles, Newton Abbot 1973.
Study of the public notice as a social instrument (and also as a mirror of its time). Proclamations, Rewards, Wanted (including 'Young girls wanted for pickling and bottling'), Caution, Rules (of prisoners), Company, Gas, Squibs, Railways (Newcastle and Carlisle).

The Valentine and its origins, Frank Staff, Lutterworth Press, London 1969; Praeger, New York 1970.
The Saturday Book No 26 ed. John Hadfield. 'Valentines' by Arthur Calder-Marshall, Hutchinson, London 1966.

The History of the Christmas Card, George Buday, R. E. Rockliff, London 1954.
The Picture Postcard and its origins, Frank Staff. Lutterworth Press, London; Praeger, New York 1966.
Pictures in the Post Richard Carline, Gordon Fraser, London 1959
Picture Postcards, Marian Klamkin, Rural Life Series 1973

Matchbox Labels of the World, A.J. Cruise, Robert Ross, London 1946.
The first book on this subject.
Match box labels, Joan Rendell, David & Charles, Newton Abbot 1968.
An Introduction to Stamp Collecting, Colin Narbeth, Arthur Barker, London 1970.
International Encyclopedia of Stamps, James Mackay, IPC, London 1971–72.
Stanley Gibbons Collector's Guide, Stanley Gibbons Publications, London 1975.
Cover collecting, James Mackay, Collecta, London 1968.
Collecting Postal History, Prince Dimitry Kandaouroff, Peter Lowe, London 1973.
This interesting and well printed book has illustrations not only of a variety of covers but also of other printed ephemera connected with the postal service.
Gibbons Simplified Stamp Catalogue (The World). Stanley Gibbons Publications, London.
Standard Postage Stamp Catalog, 5 vols., Scott Publications Inc., New York 1975.
Design in Miniature, David Gentleman, Studio Vista, London; Watson-Guptill, New York 1972.
This book by a very distinguished designer covers not only the detailed design of postage stamps, but also the design of matchbox and other labels.
Collecting Cigarette Cards, Dorothy Bagnall, London Cigarette Card Co. 1973.
The Saturday Book No 32 ed. John Hadfield 'Joys of Cartophily' by Peter Scully, Hutchinson, London 1972.

British Cigarette Card Issues 1888–1919.
Catalogue and Handbook 1973.
British Cigarette Card Issues 1920–1940.
Catalogue and Handbook 1974.
The Catalogues and Handbooks are published by the London Cigarette Card Co. London.
Bookbinding, Douglas Cockerell, Pitman, London, 4th Edition 1925.
The conservation of printed matter and methods of cleaning.

Acknowledgements

The illustrations from public collections have acknowledgements printed under them. I would like to express my appreciation to the Controller of H.M. Stationery Office and the Trustees of the British Museum and the Victoria and Albert Museum and the Bodleian Library for waiving their reproduction fees.

I want to thank Robert Wood for his generous loan of all the Hartlepool material and for much help besides; and George Arnott for his generous loan of the Woodbridge material.

I would also like to thank the following people who have helped me in many ways with information and the loan of material:

Dorothy Bagnall, Christian Barker, Hervey Benham, Messrs Jonathan Cape, Ian and Jackie Craig, Charlotte Don, Annabel Fairbrother, William Fenton, Robin Hyman, London Cigarette Card Company, George Mackie, Marlborough Fine Arts Ltd, James Mosley, Gerald Nason, John Player and Sons Ltd, Peter Probyn, Jeff Thomson, Vera Trinder Ltd (Postage Stamp Dealers), and all the artists who have allowed me to use their Christmas cards.

I am most grateful for the help I have received from various tutors and students at the Newport College of Art, the Norwich School of Art, Gray's School of Art, Aberdeen, and the Royal College of Art.

A special debt of gratitude is due to Sue Tombs who gave up her Christmas holiday to re-touch all the photographs and mount and scale the illustrations.

Finally, I would like to thank my wife, Griselda, who has helped me in a hundred different ways with the production of this book.

London and North Western, Midland, and Sheffield and Lincolnshire Railways.

Further Reduction
IN THE FARES
On and after MONDAY NEXT, February the 25th, by the

FAST TRAINS
Between the undermentioned Places and
LONDON.

UP TRAINS.		A.M.	P.M.	Fares to London 1st Class. s.	d.	2nd Class. s.	d.
York -	dep.	9 50	4 20				
Milford Junc.	,,	10 15	4 45				
Bradford -	,,	9 40	4 10	5	0	3	6
Leeds -	,,	10 15	4 45				
Wakefield via Norm.	,,	10 11	3 33				
Normanton -	,,	10 40	5 10				
Swinton -	,,	11 10	5 40	5	6	3	6
Sheffield Vic. Sta.	,,	11 0	5 30	6	0	4	0
London -	arr.	4 0	10 20				

DOWN TRAIN.		A.M.	P.M.	Fares from London 1st Class s.	d.	2nd Class s.	d.
London -	dep.	9 45	5 0				
Sheffield Vic. Sta.	arr.	2 30	9 45	6	0	4	0
Swinton -	,,	2 20	9 40	5	6	3	6
Normanton -	,,	2 55	10 10				
Wakefield via Norm.	,,	3 20	10 50				
Leeds -	,,	3 20	10 35				
Bradford -	,,	4 15	11 5	5	0	3	6
Milford Junc.	,,	3 20	10 35				
York -	,,	3 45	11 0				

NOTE.—The Fares to and from London by the above Companies' Route will in no case exceed those charged by any other Company.

By Order,

MARK HUISH,
JAS. ALLPORT,
ED. WATKIN.

Feb. 2nd, 1856.

W. Bemrose and Sons, Printers by Steam Power, Derby.

One hundred and twenty years ago the first class fare from London to York cost five shillings. At the time of writing, the fare is £9.35. Pieces of printed ephemera such as this railway notice are timely reminders of changing values. It is a salutary note on which to end this not altogether serious book.